1973-74

Reliving the NC State Wolfpack's Title Run

1973-74

Reliving the NC State Wolfpack's Title Run

BY JIM POMERANZ

CARYTOWN PRESS

Dedication

To the 1973–74 NC State University Wolfpack basketball team, its coaches, players, managers and others who were a direct part of winning the 1974 NCAA national basketball championship;

To my fellow staff members at the *Technician,* the NC State University student newspaper, especially those who tutored me as I entered the world of journalism, and to our longtime advisor A. C. Snow;

And, of course, last on this page but not the least of anyone else, to my wife of 32 years, Nancy, for her patience and encouragement. Without her, I could not have completed this journal.

—**Jim Pomeranz**

Contents

.

Foreword

Reading *1973–74 Reliving the NC State Wolfpack's Title Run* brought smiles and the reminder of a few shed tears of joy and emotion as I relived each game and the events around them during this account of the season leading to State's first national championship, the greatest time in Wolfpack basketball history. That season was the climax of the unprecedented two consecutive undefeated Atlantic Coast Conference seasons with two ACC tournament championships.

This account is an outstandingly real reminder of the life, emotions, and pride that the 1973–74 team brought not only to the student body, the university, and its alumnae, but also to Raleigh, the State of North Carolina, and the entire ACC geographic area.

Mindfully important is the knowledge that this NC State success story was preceded by a rich NC State tradition, which was significant in setting the stage for the Wolfpack's 1974 national championship. That great NC State tradition dates back to the truly accomplished and amazing coaching of Everett Case, Press Maravich, and Norm Sloan, along with prior remarkable NC State All-American players Dick Dickey, Sammy Ranzino, Vic Molodet, Ronnie Shavlik, Lou Pucillo, John Richter, and Bobby Speight, all of whom set the pattern for greatness in NC State and ACC basketball.

NC State fans of all ages, including those born since that illustrious era, will find this account fascinating and enormously enjoyable. Jim Pomeranz's journal provides a unique historical chronicle, which entertainingly also includes enlightening personal interviews with individual players and of head coach Norm Sloan, who guided NC State to win that magical national championship in the years when the challenging ACC from top to bottom was the very best in the country.

Having been a member of the coaching staff during that incredible unmatched era in NC State and ACC basketball, it was extremely enjoyable to relive those days and recount the events from a different perspective. My college coaching career began in 1969 in the recruiting of these notable players, who were coached to play the game with intelligence, intensity and skill. The bar that was set for excellence during the era of the 1973–74 team has become the driving force in how and what I demand in coaching my teams in order to have them strive to be the best they can be each game and each season.

Every team has its own storyline with serious and humorous occurrences that combine to mold a team into one unit as a season progresses. This team was no exception, but what this team also had was an abundance of excellence.

At the core of the starting lineup were three remarkable athletes: Tommy Burleson, Monte Towe, and David Thompson. At the core of this team's storyline were the ordeals and successes of Tommy Burleson, State's 7'2½" center (touted as 7'4" by the sports information director). Add the contrast of one of college's smallest point guards 5'5" Monte Towe (5'7" in the press guides), whose heart and personality were much larger than his diminutive stature.

Then there was David Thompson, who, without a doubt, was the very best non-big man that ever played college basketball. David's post-season personal interview with Jim Pomeranz revealed good insight into the quality of David's character and why he was loved by teammates and basketball fans worldwide. Having had the good fortune to come to know and admire David's family and background, I saw firsthand just why David's work ethic, character, and love of the game became so great.

But the incredible achievement of this team required that all the stars be aligned in order to attain such lofty success. Three great players would not have been enough to achieve such unparalleled team triumph. The addition of two proven winners, both great high school players, completed the starters. Tim Stoddard came to NC State as a three-sport standout from the highly regarded East Chicago Washington High School, where, as a senior, his basketball team won the state championship, and where Tim was undefeated as a baseball pitcher and was quarterback on a football team that lost only one game. And the outstanding junior college transfer Moe Rivers effectively rounded out the starting lineup, bringing experience as a superior ball-handler and great defensive player with a winning history. Those five starters were the heart of the team. They had exceptional skills, but, too, they were guided by the masterful coaching of Norm Sloan.

How fortunate to be a part of Norm Sloan's coaching staff as we battled the great teams from both the University of Maryland, led by Lefty Driesell, and UNC, led by Dean Smith. Most people remember the two epic battles with the perennial national champion UCLA, but the manner in how this team achieved nine straight victories over UNC and ten straight wins over Maryland served as the basis for my personal learning experiences for future decades in coaching.

The widely held opinion was that UCLA, NC State, Maryland, Marquette, and UNC were the best five teams in the country in the 1973–74 season. NC State won seven of eight games in those matchups that season. The 103–100 triple overtime win over #3 Maryland in the ACC tournament is still regarded by most as the best game ever played in the ACC and is certainly one I will never forget and will forever treasure.

There are endless stories to relate, but I invite you to read and enjoy this account of that magical season, thanks to Jim Pomeranz. Enjoy this different way of looking at history. Relive the greatest time in NC State basketball.

—Coach Eddie Biedenbach

Eddie Biedenbach played basketball for NC State 1965–68 and was selected first team All-Atlantic Coast Conference in 1966, playing for coach Press Maravich, and in 1968, playing for coach Norman Sloan. Those same years, Biedenbach was named to the All-ACC tournament team. In 1970, he joined Sloan's staff as an assistant, coaching the Wolfpack through the 1978 season. After three years as head coach at Davidson, he was an assistant coach for eight years at Georgia before returning to his alma mater as an assistant coach for three seasons under coach Les Robinson. In 1996, he became the head coach at UNC-Asheville and was there for 17 years after which he went to UNC-Wilmington as an assistant coach for one season. In the spring of 2014, Eddie was elected to the North Carolina Sports Hall of Fame. He remains today one of NC State's most ardent fans.

"My ride left me"

It was about 1:30 in the morning of Tuesday, March 26, 1974. I really didn't know the time and really didn't care. It was late, or early, depending on one's perspective. I was reliving what had happened a few hours prior, reflecting on what had transpired in the last six months, celebrating what seemed to be the present, and imagining what was soon to come.

Then I met someone. It was a happenchance meeting 90 minutes after midnight with a fellow NC State University student, who eventually told me he could never completely repay me for what I was about to do. It was 20 years later that he refreshed my memory of that evening (or morning), offering the exact time and the date, and reminding me of the promise that he could never completely repay what he said was a debt of gratitude.

Several hours had passed since the final buzzer of the 1974 NCAA National Basketball Championship game, won by NC State, 76–64, over Marquette. As sports editor of the State's student newspaper, the *Technician*, I had attended and covered the game in the Greensboro Coliseum, packed up my typewriter and notes, made a few rounds at parties at the Albert Pick Hotel and at the team hotel—a Holiday Inn or Ramada or something like that. At the Wolfpackers party, the fans, though not happy with me for criticizing their lock on tickets for post-season play, embraced my attendance. The team treated me like one of their own after a season of stories about games and personalities. Even head coach Norman Sloan—a usually gruff character to the media, especially the student press—was out-going, joking, and smiling, welcoming me to the celebration.

There was a stop back near the coliseum and a short visit to the media hotel where the booze flowed and the talk had turned to the next season. Then, along with a couple of other students as riders, I steered my Mercury Montego—it had ferried me back and forth from Raleigh to Greensboro not only for the last few days to cover this tournament, which included a semi-finals win over UCLA, 80–77, but also the Atlantic Coast Conference tournament two weeks earlier—up onto Interstate 40, headed east, back to Raleigh and to a party of thousands who had taken over Hillsborough Street for hours.

It was bitterly cold and a bit icy as a winter storm had hit the area a few days earlier. As we made our way up the ramp, across the bridge over High Point Road and onto I-40, we passed a hitch-hiker holding a small sign on which was hand-scribbled "RALEIGH." Never one to stop for strangers, I made an exception, bringing the car to a halt about 50 yards beyond him. He was wearing a red sweatshirt emblazoned with "NC State Wolfpack," so I knew I would be doing a fellow student a huge favor.

"Thanks," he said, smiling after running to catch up, and as he stumbled into the back seat. "My ride left me. I've got to get back to Raleigh. I have a huge test in the morning."

He told us his name, but I didn't remember it. We were all tired, so there was little conversation, if any, during the next 75 minutes. Some slept, others babbled about the title game and the accomplishments of the season. The new rider kept quiet. As we approached Raleigh, trying to enter on Hillsborough Street to drive along the northern edge of the campus and the hub of the celebration, I realized an alternate route would be better. Maneuvering through some side streets, we eventually hit Clark Avenue, turned right onto

Enterprise Street, and headed toward the Belltower. At Hillsborough Street where Sadlack's Heroes sat closed, my passengers, seeing thousands of students still in the street, decided they had had enough of the car and jumped out. My new-found friend, whose name I couldn't remember, thanked me over and over, asking what he could do to repay me for stopping just past that bridge in the freezing temperatures.

"Nothing at all," I told him. "Enjoy yourself." The doors were closed. I was tired and had no sane reason to take part in the party in front of me, so I headed down Pullen Road to Western Boulevard, Avent Ferry Road, Kings Row Apartments and my bed. I had a story to write later that day for Wednesday's edition of the *Technician*. The article for the student newspaper had nothing to do with the ride home, which I remembered but never recounted.

Twenty years later, I was reminded of the ride home after the storied season and the title-winning game. The hitch-hiker by chance found me one day, reintroduced himself, and continued to ask what he could do to repay me for stopping and offering him a ride back to campus. Nothing, I kept telling him. At the very least, he wanted to tell me what happened with the test and a professor who was unrelenting, demanding that students take his tests even amidst a celebration that the NC State University campus had never seen or experienced before.

—**Jim Pomeranz**

Introduction

During the academic year of 1973–74 at NC State University, the men's basketball team generated most of the excitement on campus. It created most of the excitement in all of Raleigh and throughout North Carolina, for that matter. The buzz created by the Wolfpack as it played its way to winning the NCAA National Championship reached far beyond athletics, helping many get past international, national, local, and campus issues of concern.

It was a trying time across the United States with the Vietnam conflict still raging. There was an energy shortage with the possibility of gas rationing. The United States presidency was in jeopardy because of the 1972 break-in of the Democratic National Committee at the Watergate complex in Washington DC and Chief Executive Richard Nixon's subsequent cover-up. These issues and others were of concern to State students, faculty, and staff as well as most United States citizens. On the NC State campus, students in general were upset that the annual All-Campus concert celebration was cancelled due to lack of funds. Campus politics was, well, campus politics. Issues on campus came and went, some lingering and others passing.

The African-American population, which made up 2.4% of total enrollment, was upset about the small number of black counselors and professors and was also upset about other related issues. We discovered from Dean of Student Affairs Banks Talley why it would be difficult for State to reach a 10% desegregation goal set forth by the University of North Carolina Board of Governors but that a 1% increase, going from 350 African-American students to 500 by 1977, could be met. "Black students are not inclined towards the hard sciences but more towards the liberal arts," he told the student newspaper, the *Technician*. "This fact is one reason for the relatively small projected black enrollment increase for State. We think there will be no problem reaching our goal. Things look encouraging this year. (But 10% black enrollment at State or Carolina is unrealistic at the present time because) there are not enough black students to go around for State and Carolina to have several thousand black students."

In many ways, it was a typical setting for nearly any college campus at that time, but State's success in athletics—especially basketball but also football and baseball—seemed, for the most part, to bring the campus together. In the fall, the football team was undefeated in the Atlantic Coast Conference, winning the league title and a Liberty Bowl game with Kansas. During the winter, the basketball team completed a second straight undefeated ACC regular season, won the league tournament for a second conference title, and won four NCAA tournament games, including the national semifinals over UCLA, to capture the national title. While the basketball team was grabbing the spotlight, the swimming team was winning its 13th ACC title and the 8th in a run of capturing 18 of 20 conference championships. And, in the spring, the baseball team, after an average regular season, won the ACC tournament played on State's home field.

Today, to those who were State students that year, the triumphant run by the Wolfpack basketball team, and the successes of football, swimming, and baseball seem more recent than the more than 40 years before the writing of this chronicle. To those who lived it, to those who closely followed the season, attended the games, and wrote about the team and games for the college newspaper, the *Technician*, the memories are not distant at all.

It seems as if it were just yesterday that David Thompson was soaring with great ease and determined intensity to the rim of the basket in Reynolds Coliseum to gather a bullet pass from Monte Towe and then casually and lightly drop the ball through the hoop. Dunking was not allowed. Watching Tommy Burleson "grow up" as a basketball player and become an inside force hard for any competitor to handle is fresh. There was Norman Sloan in his loudly plaid jacket doing his "stormin'" at courtside, demanding more from his talented team and less from the game officials.

The three times I made the short drive to Greensboro to see the Wolfpack win three tournaments—Big Four, ACC, and NCAA— remains a recent memory though it happened in January and March of 1974. Watching Monte impatiently creep to the free throw line, with cramps in his legs, to sink two charity tosses that iced the win for State against Maryland in the greatest ACC game ever played is very clear. Being amazed always but never surprised to see David leap higher than Bill Walton to gather a crucial rebound is a neat memory that seems as if it happened a day ago. The sky-hooks of Burleson, knocking in shot after shot over some of the best centers in the game, could have been as recent as the day this is being written.

The memories to those who lived it are not just memories. The memories are reality.

I lived much of the basketball season as sports editor of the *Technician*, the student newspaper. Ken Lloyd, my predecessor, gave up that position shortly after the Wolfpack football season in the fall of 1973. Ken wanted to concentrate on academics to make sure he graduated that spring. Also a senior but not having enough credit hours for 1974 graduation, I thirsted to lead the coverage of the basketball team and didn't hesitate to say yes when Beverly Privette,

10

the editor, asked me to move from assistant sports editor to Ken's seat.

Getting to know the players was not very hard, especially the juniors and seniors; most of them were college friends before the athlete-writer relationship. Being a student writer didn't put distance between us. Unlike writers, reporters, and the multitude of media types today, who are on the lookout for the tiniest possibility of impropriety, ready to send a tweet or to post a quick story on a website, our staff had unwritten rules to keep coverage to action on the court, much as did the sports writers and reporters for the daily issues in Raleigh and around the state. We were more likely to be part of the fun of being a student than to distance ourselves from the players. Conversation and activities off the court and away from the locker room were off limits for stories. Friendships and relationships made then remain today. And secrets made then remain secrets today.

The players—David, Tommy, Monte, Mark Moeller, Craig Kuszmaul, Tim Stoddard, Phil Spence, Morris Rivers, Greg Hawkins, and others—were not shielded from campus association though Coach Sloan may have wanted it just a little more than it was. These fellow students, as good as they were on the court and as much as they were worshipped by non-students, especially by members of the Wolfpack Club, were regular guys off the court. They had their fun and included other students.

On the court, the players melded into a spectacular team, rolling to a 12–0 conference record and a 30–1 overall mark. It was State's first national basketball title and the best team of two Wolfpack basketball national championship squads. There is no doubt that the 1974 championship team would consistently get the better of State's other national title team, the Jim Valvano-coached miracle Cinderella story of 1982–83. If the two squads played a 10-game series, the 1974 team would win 9 times, maybe all 10.

Probably, the 27–0 team from the previous year, 1972–73, a team on probation and not competing in the NCAA tournament, would also defeat State's second NCAA title team as many times in as many chances. Those two teams—1972–73 and 1973–74—were that good. The 1972–73 and 1973–74 Wolfpack teams combined to go 17–1 against nationally ranked opponents, including a 14–1 mark against teams ranked in the national top 10, 10–1 against teams ranked in the top 5, and 5–1 against teams ranked in the top 3. Those numbers are tough for any college team to match.

As a State student in the early 1970s and as many alumni of a lot of colleges and universities enjoy doing, I get pleasure from looking back to relive the glory of my days at State. A question asked of many usually goes something like this: Knowing what you know today, would you like to return to your college days and do it all over again? My answer is yes, but I don't have to know any more than I did then to do it all over again. Well, maybe I would about some things, but not about the fortunes of the basketball team.

This book is about 1973–74 State basketball, but it's not a "look back" manuscript. It's a look at that season in the present tense with my past tense observations. Writing a book about what happened more than 40 years ago by talking to the characters and what they are doing today is a volume for someone else. This book is based on stories and information taken directly from the student newspaper, the *Technician*, much of which I penned. The departing editor created several bound volumes of the entire year of printed newspapers and distributed them to some staff members. I was one of the lucky few to be given the 1973–74 bound edition of the *Technician*. It's something that I've read and reread countless times.

This project, which could have been completed by a number of people, began in 2002 with an idea that's pretty much as you see it here. Soon after starting the project, I expanded it to include more of the entire year at State as seen through the *Technician*. But, as the word content grew, the original idea returned. This book is about 1973–74 NC State Wolfpack basketball and winning the NCAA National Championship as seen through the writings in the *Technician*, some reprinted in their entirety as complete chapters and others included in part in other chapters. You'll read some in present tense and some in past tense. Instead of chapters about those players from today's perspective, you'll read stories about the players when they were at State. And, since there were games played when the *Technician* did not publish, details of some games are not included in this book. The articles from the *Technician* have been copy edited for correctness, clarity, and consistency using the Chicago Manual of Style 16th Edition and Merriam-Webster's Collegiate Dictionary 11th edition. Overall, the work of students during the academic year 1973-74 remains intact.

To put this chronicle into perspective, before the games begin, before the player profiles, you'll take a few steps back from the 1973–74 basketball season and explore the commitment to successful athletics at State through comments from Chancellor John Caldwell and Director of Athletics Willis Casey. And, there's a look at the NCAA probation that kept the 1972–73 Wolfpack from competing in play beyond the Atlantic Coast Conference tournament.

Closing on an interesting note, the "Postscript"—not from the *Technician*—is a lengthy interview with David Thompson, which I conducted after the completion of the season for the first *ACC Basketball Handbook* published by my longtime friend and fellow State alum Ivan Mothershead, (NCSU '70), who gave permission for its use here. The postscript is followed by "Overtime: The stuff of memories," another personal note about winning the title and being there when it happened.

Reprinted *Technician* stories and parts thereof are included with the permission of NC State University given to me in 2009 by Bradley Wilson, then the coordinator of student media at State. "You have asked for permission to reprint in part or in their entirety articles from the NCSU student newspaper, the *Technician*, from academic year 1973–74 in your book on the men's basketball team," wrote Bradley in a letter. "Certainly such use is granted for use in the book and any materials necessary to publicize the book. Please ensure that any materials from the *Technician* are attributed to the original reporter or photographer. As you said (in your request), the early 1970s were an exciting time to be at NCSU, and I'm glad you were there to document those special moments."

So am I. And I hope you enjoy reliving that special 1973–74 NC State Wolfpack basketball season as much as I've enjoyed putting it together.

— Jim Pomeranz

SECTION 1

Setting the Scene

Chapter 1

The foundation for success

Intercollegiate athletics was established to give students physical activity and to supplement academic missions. To put it mildly, intercollegiate athletics has grown to be more than that. Everything is relative; today, intercollegiate athletics is a huge business that, in many cases, seems—and maybe is—bigger in stature than the colleges and universities represented by the student teams.

An annual projected budget of $1.3 million for a major college athletics department is nonexistent in 2013–14, but that same amount in 1973–74, supporting 13 intercollegiate teams, opened eyes, especially those of the student writers at the *Technician,* State's student newspaper, and caused concern.

Rising student fees to support athletics and scholarship funds for athletics coming in part from proceeds of sales at the Student Supply Store, where books and supplies were purchased, were cause for concern. The student newspaper, in early September that year, devoted a glossy 16-page insert—*Touché*—to intercollegiate athletics. It discussed the budget, athletics in general and the role of athletics on a college campus.

In State's athletics budget, the students discovered more than $400,000 for athletics scholarships. Just under $900,000 went to operations and salaries. Of the $900,000, football's budget was

$337,000. Head coach Lou Holtz was paid a salary of $27,500 and the eight assistant coaches averaged just $14,500 annually. The budget for the basketball team was just $138,500, with Norm Sloan's salary $24,255. However, the athletics department was expected to end the year with a surplus of "between $20,000 and $80,000."

Imagine, a basketball coach in the ACC in his eighth season, with a team expected to win the national title, salaried more than 11% less than the football coach in his second season, not only at State, but also as the head of a major college program. At State, salary differences had more to do with revenue source than with athletics success.

From *Touché:*

The main source of operational revenue is, of course, football. State athletics will gross nearly $385,000 from the six away football games but will not be able to use the expected $543,500 derived from the games at Carter Stadium. All money taken in at the stadium has to be used to pay off the loan on the stadium, which was completed in 1966, and cannot be used for the operation of the athletic programs. The indebtedness is due to be paid off by the year 2004, but payment is running ahead of schedule. With continued success in football, Carter Stadium may be paid off in another 12 to 15 years and gate receipts will be able to be used for the operation of the athletic teams.

The next two primary sources of revenue were basketball ($283,000) and student fees ($215,000)—$20 a year per student—followed by television and radio revenue (just $110,000), which mostly came from televising the State-Carolina football game ($75,000). Basketball television revenue was estimated at $25,000, and the Atlantic Coast Conference and radio rights, a mere $10,000.

From *Touché:*

In conclusion, intercollegiate athletics at every university campus, and State is no exception, are beginning to feel the pinch of the rising cost of living. Athletic departments are finding it increasingly difficult and expensive to meet the costs of athletics on the scale that they exist today. It is becoming more costly to feed, house, and generally take care of the athletes, as well as hire and maintain highly competent and expanding coaching staffs. Fielding representative athletic teams is now a major financial chore.

To meet the rising cost, revenue has to be increased by any available means. Ticket prices to football games in Carter Stadium, as well as at most other college stadiums, have risen to $7.00. A possible increase in the student athletic fee has been tossed around at State in the recent past, with Athletics Director Willis Casey saying an increase is imminent.

But there is a limit to how much revenue can rise by increasing the prices, so costs have to be cut and controlled instead. A move to need-only scholarships in athletics is a step in that direction and administrators are looking into other means to decrease their expenditures. However, it appears there is no remedy to the situation in sight in the immediate future, so it looks as if students, fans, and contributors to the athletic programs will continue to feel the burden of the skyrocketing costs of intercollegiate athletics.

The growth of intercollegiate athletics, the writers of *Touché* noted, was directly related to the increased interest from spectators, moving sports from being something enjoyed by those who participate to something enjoyed by those who not only watch but pay to watch, demanding more access and better results. Bottom line, the writer said,

18

was that intercollegiate sports were now being enjoyed by millions instead of just the few who played.

From Touché:

But the impact of the spectator on athletics has a much greater effect than increased participation. For all intents and purposes, the spectator initiates "big-time" athletics. Some entrepreneur sees that money can be made from amateur sport and even more money can be made from professional sport. From that point on, sport is divided into two camps: the amateur, who participates mainly for personal satisfaction and fun, and the professional, who makes a living from sport.

Athletics on the major college level has aroused nationwide interest, mainly in the major sports such as football and basketball, and the same is true at State.

As has been the case in the past, the various issues involved in athletics have surfaced and become topics of discussion among both students and faculty. Recent occurrences demand it. Many questions have been raised concerning various aspects of athletics on the campus. The probation imposed by the NCAA on State's basketball program, the possibility of a future increase in student fees to aid athletics, the universal desire to win in competition, and the Wolfpack's skyrocketing success in the field of athletics recently will all play a role in the discussion.

State Chancellor John T. Caldwell enjoyed athletics, attending football and basketball games, usually not missing any home or away games and sometimes showing up at the non-revenue team sports events. "Athletics have become a very exciting and worthwhile part of the intercollegiate scene and life on university campus. All of the well-established institutions among the university ranks have well-developed athletics programs. Athletics add a dimension of wholesomeness and contribute to the morale of the University," Caldwell told the student newspaper.

"One aspect of a university's athletics program is that it ties in a wide range of the population, from the most sophisticated intellectual to the humblest individual," he said. "An exciting athletics program adds verve on a campus when played with reasonable success, and I don't mean championship teams necessarily. In the absence of it, one would find something missing in the life of the university. Institutions that have a championship every year just get used to that. Then everybody gets upset if they lose just two games, and that's a terrible attitude to develop."

From *Touché:*

The effect of a "reasonably successful" athletics program can often boost the image of a University within the eyes of a community, which Caldwell feels is unfortunate. "A lot of unsophisticated people in this broad public might not know any more about your university than the athletics program, and that is sometimes overrated in importance. Consequently, they judge your university solely by it, but that's an unfortunate fact of life," said Caldwell.

But some feel the "rah-rah, go" spirit is diminishing among the general student populace due to its irrelevance to the realities of the world. But Caldwell doesn't agree. "Well, I don't think it's a thing of the past. In the larger institutions, you have a much greater diversity of people on your campus, and you will have a portion of students and faculty not much interested, but the great majority will feel a kind of collegiate loyalty about the activities of the team, and want it to win, and share in its successes, which I think is good."

In 1973–74, the foundation for success was from the top down. State had the support of the chancellor, and that flowed to the athletics department and the Director of Athletics Willis Casey.

"We will continue to have a solvent and responsible program. If we don't plan to do so, then we'd better get out of intercollegiate athletics," said Caldwell.

Chapter 2

Athletics are a part of collegiate way of life

Reprinted from the Technician supplement, Touché, September 5, 1973

Throughout the years, intercollegiate athletics have grown to enormous proportions. With the rapid expansion of college programs has come the need for capable and astute administrators, for without them, athletics could easily become a detriment to the university they represent by becoming too big and devastating.

At State, athletics are in the hands of Willis Casey, who has demonstrated his ability as both a coach and an administrator. Before becoming director of athletics in 1969, he served as State's swimming coach for 22 years. He took this "non-existent" program in 1946 and quickly lifted it to national prominence, a level it still enjoys.

In addition to his coaching duties, Casey served as assistant athletics director from 1949–69, supervisor of the school's enormous athletics facilities and manager of 36 major basketball tournaments.

Although he is naturally pro-athletics, he is nonetheless noted for his honesty, frankness and common-sense approach concerning athletics. He does not pretend to believe athletics are simon-pure, but by the same token, he does not think intercollegiate sports are anywhere near as bad as some people make them out to be.

"I think anyone who works with intercollegiate athletics understands that not everything in the department of athletics is perfect," Casey noted. "There is no way it will ever be perfect. There will always be areas of criticism anytime you are doing something where you have 40- , 50- or 60,000 people judging.

"The controversial areas, such as football traffic, student seating at basketball games, the athletic fee (and the question of) scholarships, have all been debated for the 31 years I have been in intercollegiate athletics, and I am sure they will be debated for the next 31 years. You will always have pros and cons and feelings about it, but I think this is only natural.

"I think the ridiculous thing would be if people in intercollegiate athletics did not realize their problems and were not willing to take measures to try to improve them. But this is not happening in athletics all over the country, and I think we have a very healthy situation."

Casey believes athletics on a college campus provide an outlet for the student body that is attended by a majority of students. He thinks it serves the same purpose as the other extracurricular activities that are so much a part of college life.

"I think the value a student gets from athletics is the same he gets from the Friends of the College or New Arts series, or the so-called extracurricular activities. Athletics are here for the same reason we need a college union building. It's a part of the intercollegiate way of life that the average student enjoys. I understand there are some students who don't give a nickel for athletics and couldn't care less. But this is true of anything.

"I see athletics as a public relations device with the students and the friends of the university," he continues. "I think a successful athletic program has many fringe benefits. The students in general enjoy winning athletic teams, and I know the alumni and the friends of the university have already demonstrated they like winning programs.

"I don't think there is any question that in general athletics get far more space in the news media than they should when compared to the other facets of educational life. This is not done by the Department of Athletics or by the athletes; this is done by the news media. The television people aren't paying millions of dollars a year to televise college football in order to publicize it; rather, they are doing it because the people want to see it. They are going by the old law of supply and demand."

Many people have voiced the opinion that an intercollegiate athletic program takes money away from other parts of the university, money they feel could be put to better uses. But Casey takes the opposite view that athletics pay for themselves, and a successful athletic program even helps the university financially.

"Well, I'm biased because I'm in athletics, but I think a successful athletic program helps foundations in raising money for various academic ventures," he said. "It helps the university through cash donations and donations through properties and wills. Many who contribute to the university foundations or other types of contributions other than athletic contributions got their start probably with athletics. But again, I have a vested interest in athletics, and I am biased in my views, just like the people who think athletics are detrimental to the university."

With all the money pouring into college athletic programs, particularly football and basketball, the college game has been accused of reeking with professionalism. Many feel that the athletes who get their education free of charge are not truly amateurs, who compete for the love of competition. Again, Casey believes this view is not entirely fair.

"If our athletes are not amateurs, then I do not want a son who is a professional athlete," he stated. "If you took a full scholarship and broke down the number of hours a football player played and

24

practiced and figured what he made an hour, it would be below the federal minimum wage, I'm sure. It certainly is no lucrative thing."

During the past decade, college athletics have grown immensely, probably due a great deal to the increased demands placed on teams by fans, alumni and students. With this raises the question: Can intercollegiate athletics get too big, to a point that they are a detriment to the university?

"I think athletics could get too big anytime a program got to the point it was dictating its own rules and regulations and deciding what it was going to do and how it was going to do it," states Casey. "That would be too big for me, as a program must always be under institutional control. It should never have a win at any cost philosophy—it should aspire to have the best possible team under the restrictions placed on it by the institution."

One of the biggest complaints that students have concerning athletics is that their interests are pushed aside in favor of the interests of the Wolfpack Club, the department's fund-raising organization. However, Casey thinks the Wolfpackers are entitled to some special privileges, because through their contributions they make athletic scholarships possible.

"I don't think the students get pushed aside, but that would depend on what context you ask the question in," he said. "Without successful teams, there would be little desire on the part of the student body to attend athletic contests, and there would be no problem with seating, because there would be little demand for seats.

"To have a successful program, you have to have scholarships, and the only way you are going to raise money for them is through the Wolfpackers." Casey continues. "We have to be able to offer them something in return for their contribution other than the fact that we are going to have a good team. If they are going to give $1000, then they would like an opportunity to see the teams play.

"With success there is not only a demand from the students for tickets, but also from the alumni and the Wolfpackers. Our big problem, obviously, is in basketball, because in football we have enough seats to take care of the problem. In basketball, only about 25% of the Wolfpackers, if that many, can buy tickets to the games. So they are in the same predicament the students are in.

"The students receive a far greater benefit in football, because through the alumni and their contributions, we were able to construct Carter Stadium," the athletics director said. "In old Riddick Stadium, 50% of the students had to sit in the end-zone bleachers. So though we have a bad situation in basketball, as does about every school in the country, we have a very good situation in football. I don't think there is a school in the country that is even fairly successful in basketball that doesn't have the exact same problems as we have here. With success, you have ticket problems, but without ticket problems, you have financial problems. So I think the better of the two is to have ticket problems and to try and solve those and not have financial problems."

Much controversy has been created by the talks of an increased athletics fee, which, at $20 per year, is one of the lowest in the Consolidated University system. Casey feels an increase in the fee is imminent, for the simple fact that the costs of operating an athletic program are skyrocketing.

"In principle, I am against all fees," he remarked. "But no matter how you feel about them, they seem to be a necessity in order to operate, not only in athletics, but also in other departments of the university. I can see nothing but an increase in fees in general, because the cost of living is going up."

Casey would like nothing better than for the athletic department to get away from all outside support, particularly from the Student Supply Store. Presently, the department gets 40 % of the profits from the store for scholarships.

"I think that the people who do not approve of intercollegiate athletics, who do not think they serve any purpose, have a legitimate complaint about the profits from the Students Supply Stores going to athletic scholarships," he stated. "I could argue the point with them, but I think the simplest solution would be if we did not have to depend on the Supply Store profits for any money for scholarships."

Once the money for scholarships is obtained, the problem then arises on how to distribute the wealth. The revenue sports—football and basketball—naturally receive the most money, while the other sports have to get by with limited funds.

"It's not a question of deciding which sports get the most money," said Casey, "but rather a question of deciding which sports get how much money. Obviously, football, because of the numbers it takes to have a team, gets the lion's share of the scholarships. Basketball is limited by conference action to only 20 men.

"In all the other sports, we will give scholarship aid to any boy in any sport who we consider to be a blue-chipper, within the limitations of the total budget, which we set up each year for athletics. The sport that ranks behind football and basketball in scholarships is swimming, the reason being that we are able to get blue-chip swimmers because we have a national reputation in the sport. We are now giving scholarship aid in every sport we have, except lacrosse."

There are those who feel someone in the athletic department was not doing his job when the violations that put the State basketball team on probation occurred. However, Casey firmly believes to the contrary.

"There was no way anyone could have been aware of them (the violations). Even the coaches did not think at the time that they were violations," he said. "If I spot any violations, I immediately call the (ACC) commissioner's office and report the violation and the steps we are taking to correct it. Normally, that is the end of it. By violations I mean violations of a technical nature, not a moral one.

"We are operating under hundreds of rules and interpretations, and it's awfully hard to guard against all of them," he continues. "We are not only responsible for the athletic department, but also for the alumni, for the faculty, for the staff, and for anyone who is interested in the athletics program and does anything with our knowledge. Any actions taken in connection with athletics we are held responsible for by the NCAA and the ACC. There can be a lot of honest mistakes, and they are made every day, but we report them and take steps to see that they don't happen again."

Chapter 3

The probation of 1972–73

In the fall of 1972, the NCAA Committee on Infractions reported to the NCAA Council on an investigation of alleged violations by State. On October 24, 1972, the NCAA Council determined State had 8 violations of 6 recruiting rules:

- During the summer 1970, three prospective student-athletes served as counselors in the summer basketball camp operated by the university's head basketball coach; these three young men had just completed their senior years in high school and therefore were ineligible to serve as counselors under the association's summer camp interpretations.

- During the summer 1970, the university awarded financial assistance to two prospective student-athletes in order for the young men to attend the second session of the institution's summer school.

- During August 1970, a representative of the university's athletic interests transported a prospective student-athlete between his home and the institution's campus and was reimbursed by the university for the cost of this transportation.

- During May 1971, a representative of the university's athletic interests transported three prospective student-athletes between their homes and the institution's campus and was reimbursed by the university for the cost of this transportation.

- On June 13, 1971, a prospective student-athlete was transported to the university's campus by a representative of the university's athletic interests in order to attend freshman orientation. This was the second visit at the expense of a university athletic representative. After it was determined that he was not eligible for the orientation, he remained on the campus for five days staying cost free in a dormitory room, which was utilized at that time to house counselors in the summer basketball camp operated by the university's head basketball coach.

- While working at a summer job during the period July 31–August 6, 1971, a prospective student-athlete stayed cost free in a university dormitory room which was utilized at that time to house counselors in the summer basketball camp operated by the University's head basketball coach.

- During the period August 1–6, 1971, an assistant basketball coach participated in at least one informal basketball game with five prospective student-athletes, during which these young men revealed, demonstrated, and displayed their abilities in the sport of basketball,

- On August 6, 1971, a prospective student-athlete was transported cost free from the university's campus (site of a summer camp) to his hometown in an automobile used in the summer basketball camp operated by the university's head basketball coach.

The NCAA Council, in its decision, said "the head basketball coach and an assistant coach were in a position to prohibit or avoid" the violations. State would serve one-year probation from that date, and during that year, "the university's intercollegiate basketball team shall end its season with the playing of the last, regularly scheduled, in-season game, and it shall not be eligible to participate in any post-season basketball competition."

The post-season competition was in reference to the NCAA tournament and the National Invitation Tournament. The Atlantic Coast Conference tournament was considered part of the regular season.

There are some who believe the probation was unnecessary and was the result of Chancellor Caldwell's insistence, after talking to the head basketball coach and other athletics department personnel, to the NCAA that State did nothing wrong. Many felt that if State's administrators had admitted guilt, wrists would have been slapped and the Wolfpack would have not faced probation.

Caldwell addressed recruiting in general and the probation in particular in the interview in the early September 1973 *Touché:*

> "It is too bad there is the intensified high-pressure recruiting of particular athletes," said Dr. Caldwell. "To me this is the only negative flavor I find in the intercollegiate athletics programs. I think it's too bad that these athletes in their (high school) senior year get courted so much and have so much of their time taken up by recruiters, but some of it is their own fault. They could stop some of it themselves, but they and their parents kind of like some of it.
>
> "Nothing keeps these young men from making a decision about where to go to school, and before the recruiting season is over, they really learn a whole lot about life, and about

themselves, and their values, and what they want, and they wind up making the decision they want to make," Caldwell said. "I like our people who are recruiting to be absolutely honorable, and I have never had any reason to think that we weren't absolutely honorable in our recruiting.

"Don't let anything about that happening (last year) in the NCAA (make a) mistake (of) what we have done here. There's nothing we were charged with here in the allegations that were anything more than technical interpretations of circumstances that even bordered on the ridiculous for the most part, but, nevertheless, we drew the probation."

Caldwell feels there was no way out of the verdict due to the long list of allegations and what he calls, "being tried by his accuser."

Prior to handing down the findings about State and issuing the probation decree, the NCAA was in a dilemma because of another ACC member accused of similar recruiting violations. Even if Wolfpack coaches and administrators had admitted guilt, hoping for a slap on the wrist, the decision on State probably had to mirror the conclusion placed on the other school.

It is widely known that the violations were centered, in part, on the recruitment of David Thompson, a target for more than one college. During much of the same time State was on probation, Duke University was on NCAA probation, also for the recruiting of Thompson. In Duke's case, the NCAA found that a booster transported Thompson from his home to Greensboro in March 1971, paying for tickets to the ACC basketball tournament. A booster also drove Thompson from his home to Charlotte and purchased a sport coat, a pair of slacks, and a shirt and tie for him. The NCAA said Duke's head coach Bucky Waters and an assistant should have known about the booster and prevented the infractions. Duke's probation started August 17, 1972, about five weeks prior to State's sentence.

A year after the probations, both State's and Duke's cases were reviewed, and the restrictions were lifted. Practice for 1973–74 was soon to start. State had Thompson; Duke didn't.

Chapter 4

The foundation of State basketball

The foundation of the 1973–74 championship started when Tommy Burleson chose to matriculate at State. His decision to attend State was instrumental in David Thompson's arrival a year later. Tommy was a freshman in 1970–71 and not much more than a tall man on the court, playing only on the freshman team. In his junior year, he played to a level everyone, including Coach Norman Sloan, had wished and hoped.

In 1971–72, as a sophomore, Burleson lagged behind senior center Paul Coder much of the season. Coder had the fire and experience; Tommy, gangly and unpolished, needed to add a little weight to his skinny frame and hone his basketball skills. The same season, Thompson played on the freshman squad and performed at a higher level, more like a seasoned college player. He was the real deal, and everyone, especially the students, knew it.

The freshmen team played prior to the varsity games. Students were admitted by showing student identification cards, lining up in front of Reynolds Coliseum at least two hours before the freshman games to secure front-row, side-court seats. Rarely did anyone stay seated to watch David Thompson, along with Monte Towe and others, dominate the opposition. And, sometimes, once the freshmen were finished, the crowd thinned a little. The varsity was just 16–10 overall and 6–6 in the ACC that season.

The freshmen lost only one game that season, an away game at North Carolina. In the return bout at State, in Reynolds Coliseum, Thompson, who fouled out with 10 minutes to go in the game, scored 48 points in the Wolfpack payback, 75–45 (yes, 3 fewer points than Thompson scored). After that game, State students spilled onto the court, raising Thompson to their shoulders to carry him on victory laps around the court.

In 1972–73, the probation year, everything clicked for the Wolfpack. The team came into focus. Burleson played up to his junior potential. Thompson flourished in an up-tempo, inside-outside game. The supporting cast included Monte Towe at the point and Joe Cafferky at the second guard position. State was 27–0 and seemed very much on a mission that season to do what it could to diminish the NCAA penalty. Thompson and Burleson played in the World University Games after the season. Prior to the 27–0 run, in the summer of 1972, Burleson was a member of the USA Olympic team that was cheated out of a gold medal.

As the 1974–73 academic year started, Ken Lloyd, the *Technician* sports editor, reviewed the previous year in State sports in a late August issue of the *Technician*. About the basketball team, he wrote the following:

> In basketball, as has been said before, 27–0 tells it all. Coach Norm Sloan's cagers were touted before the season as being good, but everyone knows UCLA is the only team in the country that is supposed to go undefeated. Well, the Wolfpack, led by the incomparable David Thompson, stumped the critics and doubters by rising to the occasion repeatedly and mowing down opponent after opponent on the way to the ACC title. On more than one

occasion, the Pack had to make miraculous comebacks to pull the game out of the fire. State wound up second in both polls to UCLA.

Thompson wowed everyone who saw him, and even many who didn't, on his way to becoming a consensus All-American while only an 18-year-old sophomore. Towering Tom Burleson joined Thompson on the All-ACC team while dapper Sloan grabbed ACC coach of the year honors and was runner-up to the legendary John Wooden of UCLA for the national award.

The only point to dim the glitter of the basketball season was the one-year probation on the program. But with all but two of the top 11 players returning, State's chance at the national title may come this year.

With the 11, there were 6 recruits, 4 freshmen with impressive high school credentials, and 2 junior college transfers, who were being counted on to immediately figure into Norm Sloan's game plan.

Chapter 5

New recruits promise to add to already strong Wolfpack

Reprinted from the Technician, October 24, 1973

By Jim Pomeranz

Staff Writer

Football season is only half over, but if you pass by Carmichael Gym just about any afternoon around 4 or 5 o'clock, you may get the impression that football was over long ago. As of October 15, basketball season all over the country got underway.

State head coach Norm Sloan has his charges practicing 4 times a week in preparation for the excitement-filled upcoming basketball campaign. Along with home-and-home dates with the 6 Atlantic Coast Conference foes, the Pack faces such noted powers as Purdue, Davidson, and, of course, UCLA, the nation's number one team for 7 straight years. And if all goes as expected, State may face runner-up Memphis in New Orleans at the Sugar Bowl tournament.

So, the 1973–74 basketball season poses a few challenges for the Wolfpack, and Sloan knows it. "We'll definitely have to be improved to successfully defend our ACC championship," he said. "Although we were undefeated last year, we had several close games with conference teams, and they'll all be stronger."

But State had a strong recruiting year to replace the loss of forward Rick Holdt and guard Joe Cafferky, though the absence of the two leaders will be felt.

Six players have signed grants-in-aid to attend State and play basketball. "We feel that we've had a good recruiting year," said Sloan, "and we're very pleased these young men have decided to further their education at NC State."

Trying out as freshmen will be Bruce Dayhuff of Walkerton, IN, Ken Gehring of Akron, OH, Bill Lake of Carmel, IN, and Mike Buurma of Willard, OH. Junior college transfers Morris Rivers of Brooklyn, NY, and Phil Spence of Raleigh will also be added to the Wolfpack.

"They are all excellent basketball prospects, and we think some of them will be of immediate help," continued Sloan. But the 1973 ACC Coach of the Year does not know which ones will give quick aid. That will not be determined until "they're evaluated on the playing floor against college competition."

Dayhuff, a 6'2" guard, sports the highest scoring average of the 6, with a 29.3 point pace his senior season. Over a 4-year high school career, he averaged 21.2 points and was named to both the Indiana all-star team and to the Indiana Academic All-America 5.

Buurma, a 6'10" center, was such a standout at Willard High that his jersey was retired at the conclusion of his senior campaign. He averaged 23.7 points and 13.4 rebounds last year, and that earned him the UPI Player of the Year Award in Ohio 2-A ranks. He also was voted to the Northern Ohio League all-star team for 3 consecutive years.

Lake was another academic All-America, as well as a member of the Sunkist/Coach & Athlete Top 100 team. He led his high school to 3 straight sectional titles. The 6'11" postman owns a 16.9 career scoring average and an 11.6 rebound mark.

With a shooting accuracy from the field of a fine 55.3%, Gehring, a 6'9" forward, was recently selected to receive the coveted Citizenship Award in the Akron area. He averaged 15.0 points, 13.1 rebounds and 4 blocked shots per game in his high-school career.

Both Rivers and Spence were named to the Junior College All-America squad last season. Rivers, a 6'1" guard, averaged 16 points per game at Gulf Coast Community College in Florida, while Spence, a 6'8" forward, sparked perennial junior college power Vincennes to a 28–5 record. Spence averaged 19.2 points and 15.0 rebounds per game.

Sloan says the practices thus far could not be any better. "Their (the players) condition is great, and their attitude is great," he commented. "We have great depth for all positions, and this makes for a strong feeling for each other. We definitely have a close-knit team, and this is good."

However, Sloan does think "practice starts too early. Since it is such a long time before the first game, we will only have practice 4 times a week," he said. "But we will have 6 intra-squad games to keep us going. These give the new players a chance to learn the system."

The Red and White games will be played in Charlotte, Shelby, Asheville, Greensboro, Rocky Mount, and Raleigh. The Reynolds Coliseum appearance will be at 5:15 p.m. November 24 after the Wake Forest football game.

The Pack basketball team will once again be centered on 3 outstanding players: David Thompson, Tommy Burleson, and Monte Towe. "Those 3 will definitely be in the starting lineup," said Sloan.

But after a 27–0 season can State get any better? "We have a better team this year," said the head coach. "The only way to fail is to rely on last year. This year's team will have to make their own place."

Just like last year, Sloan thinks there is no team in the ACC that can go undefeated, even the Wolfpack, because there are too many fine teams. "We have 12 extremely important games," he said about the conference match-ups. "The team that finishes first in the regular season gets the first place bye in the tournament."

Many people wonder about the Pack's chances against UCLA in the St. Louis contest. Sloan ranks that game the 13th most important one all season behind the 12 conference games. "I think it's fine we have a chance to play such a team as UCLA. But we have to remember it has no effect on the ACC tournament seeding. We will not be uptight about it, and it will not choke us up."

State opens up the 1973–74 season with an exhibition game against the Athletes in Action on December 1.

Football season is not over yet, but just happen by Carmichael Gym some afternoon and watch the nationally ranked Wolfpack basketball team prepare for what will be a most exciting, action-packed season.

Chapter 6

Sloan sees move as beneficial to players

Reprinted from the Technician, October 31, 1973

By Ken Lloyd

Sports Editor

Although his decision to drop State's junior varsity basketball program has been met with mixed reactions, Coach Norman Sloan maintains the move is "best for all concerned" and does not "see anything constructive about having the junior varsity program."

"Bobby Knight at Indiana University did away with his junior varsity program last year and thought it was one of the best things they ever did," said Sloan. The Hoosiers made it to the NCAA finals last season.

However, the other 3 coaches of Big Four schools plan to keep their junior varsity teams and consider them an integral part of their programs. Carolina's Dean Smith said he will keep his junior varsity because "it is important to involve as many students as possible in the overall athletics program."

Sloan, on the other hand, sees many advantages in the move but takes exception with a recent newspaper account that quoted him as saying the main reason behind the decision was the embarrassment jayvee ball causes those involved.

"It's true it is embarrassing for a scholarship player to play on the junior varsity, but that was only one of the reasons," he said.

"The primary reason was I thought it would give every player on the team a better chance to be a varsity player," continued Sloan. "He wouldn't be confused as to where he stood. He wouldn't be thinking in terms of junior varsity but strictly in terms of playing varsity ball."

In addition, Sloan said he didn't "feel the junior varsity competition was good enough for our players to really benefit by it. I thought at times it was so weak it worked in the reverse. They could do things that were unsound fundamentally and get away with it. You don't want that kind of competition for a training program.

"So I felt the move would benefit our players as far as being varsity players," said Sloan, "and that is the ultimate objective of the program anyhow."

With no jayvee games preceding the varsity games, other teams on campus will have a chance to play in the preliminary games. Sloan sees this as a positive reason for dropping the junior varsity program.

"It will give increased opportunity for intramural teams to play in the preliminary games," said the coach. "The Girls' Basketball Club could use some of those preliminary games, and that would give them some exposure before the crowd. It would also give us an opportunity to have some wrestling matches, which would expose the wrestling program to a larger crowd than they would normally get."

Sloan said another reason behind the move is that it will lead to smaller teams and thus fewer scholarships. "Ultimately, I want to cut the number of people on scholarship to 15 anyhow. I don't see any point of carrying 18 on scholarship. I would rather have 14 to 15, so everybody knows he is playing, and everyone's happy. A playing player is a happy player."

Since there are 18 players on scholarship and only 15 will dress out for the games, there could be a morale problem with those who do not get to suit up. In addition, last season only 8 to 10 players were used in many of the games. Thus, many players this year will be laboring mostly on the bench.

"I am sure the 3 who do not dress out for the varsity will be unhappy about it," said Sloan. "I would be surprised if they weren't, and, as a matter of fact, I would be disappointed in them if they weren't. But I don't think it can be as devastating as everyone playing junior varsity ball."

Sloan contends it will be no more embarrassing for a player not to dress out or play much than to have him play on the junior varsity. "Last year, we had a player who became very upset and was at the point, I thought, of quitting school because he was on the junior varsity," he said.

Under the new set up, a walk-on will have a difficult time earning a spot on the team since he will not have a chance to prove himself under game conditions. He will have to shine on preseason practice.

"It does not necessarily cut out the walk-on," said Sloan. "Any young man who comes in and asks for an opportunity to play will be given an opportunity to try out."

Sloan believes that any non-scholarship player that has the ability to play will surface even without junior varsity experience. He cites Al Heartley, a walk-on who was captain of the varsity in 1971, as an example.

"Al Heartley didn't learn to play basketball on the freshman team," said Sloan. "He was a good player when he came here, or he would never have made the team."

Chapter 7

Probation: Was State's basketball program really hurt?

Reprinted from the Technician, November 28, 1973

By Jim Brewer

Staff Writer

On October 24, 1972, a shadow of gloom, descended on the NC State basketball program in the form of a one-year probation by the NCAA. But instead of rolling over and playing dead, the Wolfpack went on to have a 27–0 season.

And now over a year later, the team seems to be ready to start where they left off. Saturday night, the Wolfpack will open the season against Athletes in Action, and on December 15, the Pack will meet the UCLA powerhouse in a long awaited matchup.

With this exciting future ahead, one would think happiness would flow in the streets. But this is not the case, for there is still the question of damage done to State's basketball program lingering in people's minds.

One basketball critic (Richard Starnes), in *The Chronicle of Higher Education*, has charged that probation probably cost State $100,000 in gate receipts and TV money had the Pack played in the NCAA finals.

Others wonder about the effect probation has had on alumni donations and recruiting.

According to athletic director Willis Casey, these fears have no grounds, and the damage to the Wolfpack by probation has been minimal.

With regard to alumni gifts, Casey said, "probation doesn't enter into it—one way or the other—it doesn't hurt. In fact," stated Casey, "the Raleigh drive of the Wolfpack Club went up almost 200% to almost $200,000."

He was also quick to point out that the $100,000 referred to by Starnes was laced with a lot of maybes and ifs. To press the point, Casey then asked, "What did being 27–0 earn for us this year? Anything we might have lost by not going to the NCAA we will recoup 4 to 1 this year by having a 27–0 record last year."

Assistant basketball coach Eddie Biedenbach, who does much of the recruiting, also feels that damage to the basketball program has been slight. He felt that his job as a recruiter had not been made harder by probation. He said, "No, I haven't noticed any effect. Occasionally a boy will have a question you will have to explain, but you have to do that anyway. If you can't explain, then you may lose the prospect."

Director Casey stated that he thought the NCAA was pursuing a "get tough" policy with recruiting violations. Biedenbach said that he thought this was true, but added, "I like all the NCAA rules, although I think they will find that some of it is nit-picking." He cited one rule that prevents a recruiter from paying for a prospect's meal. "It makes you feel bad to have to split a check with a potential recruit," he said.

When questioned about the possible use of the probation incident by other schools to aid in securing an athlete, Biedenbach responded by saying, "I don't think the coaches in this league would do that, they're too high class for that sort of thing. When recruiting, we never talk about another school—we try to sell NC State." Assistant coach Biedenbach indicated that he thought this attitude has "rubbed off on the other schools."

So according to the men who should know, the Wolfpack basketball program is alive and breathing well. Meanwhile, students, faculty, and alumni wait for proof when the season opens Saturday.

SECTION 2

Playing the Games

Chapter 8

Cagers begin new season against Athletes in Action

Reprinted from the Technician, November 29, 1973

By Jim Pomeranz

Assistant Sports Editor

When the number two nationally ranked Wolfpack basketball team takes to the hardwood tomorrow night against the Athletics in Action, a new year will begin on the road to Greensboro.

Greensboro is the sight of two tournaments in which State will play this year, and one tournament in which the Pack hopes to earn a berth. The first two, of course, are the Big Four tournament and the Atlantic Coast Conference tournament. The latter of the two will decide the ACC champion and an NCAA playoff spot.

The third tournament in Greensboro is the national finals. But to get there, State will first have to win the ACC and the Eastern Regional, which will be held in Reynolds Coliseum.

So the goals that evaded the Wolfpack last year due to probation are set and ready to be accomplished.

State head coach Norm Sloan sees a definite goal for the Pack as the season rapidly approaches. "Coming in first in the ACC regular season is our main goal right now," he said. "By doing that, it will only take two games to win the conference championship.

"All in all, it's going to be a tough year," Sloan said. "You'll be very surprised with Clemson and Wake Forest. They are going to be the surprise teams of the conference."

Last year, the Wolfpack had a perfect 27–0 record, and Sloan thinks that should have never happened. "You don't go through a conference schedule like ours and expect to go undefeated," the 1951 State graduate explained.

"And this is a whole new year," Sloan continued. "Everyone keeps trying to tie last year and this year together, but you can't. It's a different year, a different season."

State's team is a different one from last year, but it has the same nucleus. Leading the way for the Pack will be All-American David Thompson. Last year as a sophomore, he averaged 24.7 points per game and 21 points per game in the University World Games last summer. Sloan calls him the "the greatest athlete I've ever known."

At a point 12" higher than Thompson and playing in the pivot will be tall Tom Burleson. He played on the 1972 Olympic team and also on the 1973 University World Games team, which decked Russia for the title. In last year's ACC tourney, Burleson was named Most Outstanding Player and the winner of the Everett Case Award.

Almost 2' below Burleson at guard is State's Mighty Mite, Monte Towe. Last year, the small All-American proved, beyond a doubt, that there is still a place for the little man in major college basketball. Only 5'7", the little guy was the third leading scorer on last year's team, with 10 points per game.

The core of last year's team is back, but this year the Pack will be without the services of guards Joe Cafferky and Rick Holdt, who were lost to graduation. But filling in for the two will be two capable players.

Filling in for Cafferky will be 6'1" Morris Rivers from Brooklyn, NY, who comes to State from Gulf Coast Junior College where he was an All-American and conference Player of the Year. Sloan said he will "never try to compare" Rivers to Cafferky but did say that "Rivers will be one of the finest players in college basketball."

A player who saw plenty of action at forward last year as a sophomore behind Holdt has gained the starting role this year. Junior Tim Stoddard played last year in the substitute role, but soon after the opening buzzer, he was in the game as a very important addition. He averaged almost 8 points per game coming off the bench and pulled down over 5 rebounds per game.

Rounding out State's basic 10 players will be seniors Steve Nuce and Greg Hawkins, juniors Mark Moeller and Craig Kuszmaul, and sophomore Phil Spence. Nuce, Hawkins, Moeller, and Kuszmaul all saw action as reserves last year.

Spence comes to State from Vincennes Junior College and will be battling for a forward spot with Stoddard and Nuce. As a freshman at Vincennes he averaged 19.2 points and 15 rebounds per game on his way to All-America honors. Spence is a Raleigh native and played at Broughton High School.

Chapter 9

Athletes 'inspire' State in 119–82 romp

Reprinted from the Technician, December 3, 1973

By Jim Pomeranz

Assistant Sports Editor

For approximately the first 12 minutes of play Saturday night, before 11,300 avid Wolfpack fans in Reynolds Coliseum, State's basketball team looked as if it were going to help the Athletes in Action win their second game of the season.

Bad passes by Wolfpack players along with sharp shooting by the AIA kept the game close throughout the entire first half, with 13 points being the largest margin State could ever muster. Midway through the initial period, the Athletes even held a 2-point lead over the Wolfpack.

With Norm Sloan's troops nursing only a 10 point lead at the halftime break, the AIA players, who are workers for the Campus Crusade for Christ, expounded on their relationship with Christ before the crowd. It's not known for sure if the Wolfpack players were inspired by the proceedings, but they came out in the second half and outscored the Athletes 3 times over in the first 9 minutes to take a commanding 90–55 lead.

After that it was all downhill (for AIA) as the Pack hit 65% of its shots in the second half, as compared with 45% in the first period, to win the game, 119–82.

State has scheduled AIA for the last three years and this year was a little different than the other two. "Athletes in Action played real well," said Sloan after the game. "They're a much improved ball club over last year's team. I'm real glad we scheduled them."

Sloan said he thought the game was a good experience for State at this time in the season. "It helped us a lot," he said. "We had the opening game jitters, even though it was not officially our opener, and it let us learn some of the things we need to work on."

Leading the way for the Pack was All-America David Thompson with 34 points and 8 rebounds and Tom Burleson with 32 points and 17 rebounds. "Tommy played very well," commented Sloan, "and David played well, as expected."

After removing the top Wolfpack players and replacing them with reserves, Sloan said he was "very impressed" with the play of freshman guard Bruce Dayhuff. "He did things for us," said the head mentor in his eighth year at State. "He did a fine job. He was loose and relaxed and had his head up."

The problems in the first half, Sloan said, were also due to State's defensive play. "We were a little ragged there," he explained. "But we show promise of being a good defensive ball club."

Little Monte Towe, who scored 10 points and escaped with 13 big rebounds, said a combination of things kept the game close in the first half. "When things began to open up for us," he said, "they would start hitting and pull up. There were many things together. We weren't hitting the boards."

Burleson, who played as if he were the only player on the court, controlling the boards and blocking shots, gave credit to the slow start to the opening game of the season. "We were experimenting and putting things together," Burleson said. "They were good, and we were not playing well."

Chapter 10

Success brings changes and controversy

With the start of basketball season, it was learned that a no-alcoholic-beverages policy for Reynolds Coliseum, unless authorized by the chancellor, was in place, mirroring the guidelines set earlier that year for Carter Stadium. The littering of the coliseum with bottles and cans and a State law forbidding alcohol consumption at athletics events were part of the reasoning for the new rule.

The campus beverage policy, as reported by staff writer Howard Barnett in the December 3 edition of the *Technician,* "remains the same overall, permitting the possession and consumption of beverages of less than 14% alcohol by those of sufficient legal age anywhere on campus except in any room being used for instructional purposes. It also permits the possession and consumption of beverages of more than 14% alcohol in the rooms of those of legal age and in other rooms if the chancellor shall so designate."

The legal age of alcohol consumption was 18. Head of campus security Bill Williams, speaking about the new policy for Reynolds Coliseum, said, "We've been needing it for a long time."

In the Letters sections of the November 30 and December 3 issues of the *Technician,* there was a small scuffle about the appointment of student managers for the basketball squad.

Six students—senior Danny Smith; juniors Tony Congleton, Darryl A. Kelley, and Mark Hitchcock; and sophomores Frank Dimmock and John A. K. Tucker—were quoted in the November 30 edition, titled "All in the family:"

First of all, we would like to say that we have had a lot of respect and pride for the State athletic program. But something has come to our attention, and we think something should be said. It appears that there is a little conflict about who should be the managers on this year's Wolfpack basketball squad. Now you understand that a manager is just a glorified water boy, and that in itself isn't much. What makes the manager's job so valuable is that he travels with the team to all the away games (like the UCLA game in St. Louis). Our beef concerns the choosing of these managers. There were three students in the running for these positions: a former JV player, Mike Sloan, and David Gardner. The coaching staff decided that the team required only two managers, so one had to be let go. The former basketball player deserves to have one of the positions. The two contenders for the final spot are David Gardner, a senior, who was in line for the head manager's position, and Mike Sloan, a junior, who transferred from Carolina this year. David was manager on last year's squad, and Mike, as his name might suggest, is the son of coach Norman Sloan. Mike Sloan was picked over David. We feel that this is not fair at all. That's pretty dirty to choose one's own son over someone who has given his valuable time to the team in the past. David was sure looking forward to the travels with this year's squad, but it looks like Stormin' Norman is keeping it in the family.

The rebuttal came from Neil Edwards, printed in the December 3 issue, "Not unreasonable:"

A letter appearing in the Friday, November 30 edition of the Technician discussed the appointment of Mike Sloan (Norm Sloan's son) as head manager of the Wolfpack basketball team and the decision by the coaches to dismiss Dave Gardner. Gardner managed last year. Sloan did not. Gardner apparently feels he should have gotten the head managing position because of that fact. As a former manager of the team myself, I will not try to justify coach Sloan's decision. I do not think the coach needs to justify his decisions on any matters concerning the team. I must, however, clarify one thing. The only information the managers of last year's team were given concerning the selection of a new head manager was that coach Sloan would make the decision. Coach Sloan did exactly that, so I fail to see where Mr. Gardner, myself, or anyone else was wronged. As far as the qualifications of Mike Sloan are concerned, just drop by Reynolds Coliseum for practice any day, and you'll see that he and his assistant Biff Nichols are doing a good job. It you don't believe your eyes, ask the ballplayers or the men who work in the cage downstairs. I think it is unfortunate that a person could do as good a job as Mike does and still be the target of such unfeeling and unknowing critics as those who complained to the Technician. In summary, the coach may not always be right, but the coach is always the coach. Norm Sloan is THE COACH, a good one. Mike Sloan is THE MANAGER, a good one.

It was also time—just prior to exams and Christmas break—for students to place orders for the Atlantic Coast Conference basketball tournament scheduled for early March. Students had to pay a $25 deposit at the time of signing up for one of 200 tickets allotted to State students. The school received more than 2,000, which would be offered to Wolfpack Club members and used for university officials. State, the year before, was one of three ACC schools that offered tournament tickets to students. Duke and Virginia were the other two. Only 182 students ordered tickets for the 1973 tournament. Frank Weedon, assistant athletics director, said, "We need to get it done early and know how many tickets will be taken (by students)." He explained that tickets not bought by students would go to the Wolfpack Club to sell to its members.

The editorial writers at the Technician didn't think much of the early sale period. In the December 5 edition, there was an editorial titled "Ticket to ride:"

> Students who care to witness the Wolfpack's basketball fortunes in post-season play, that is, the Atlantic Coast Conference tournament in Greensboro, are required to make their plans now. It really couldn't come at a more inopportune time.
>
> Students will be allotted 200 of the 2,000 tournament tickets given to the school. It goes without question that the Wolfpack Club will get the other 1800. That, however, is something that seems unchangeable since it has always been this way and will always be this way. The men with the money are the ones who are favored by the athletic department. This system is debatable, but deaf ears are normally turned on the students by the department.
>
> But to ask students to enter a lottery for the tournament tickets three months ahead of the ACC tournament just so the Wolfpack Club can get their hands on the tickets the students don't want is asking a little too much. An attempt is being made to appear generous. After all, nobody has to give the students even 200 tickets. Nobody has to give them even one ticket.

At any rate, these minor injustices aside, these are rather inopportune times for students to be given the opportunity to register for the tournament tickets. The State-UCLA game in St. Louis and the Liberty Bowl in Memphis are just on the horizon, and many of the students who attend these two events will also want to attend the ACC tournament.

So large expenses are already being incurred by these two games, plus Christmas is also near, causing further strain on the student pocketbook, which is notoriously slim anyway. Add to all this the fact that students must pay $25 for the opportunity to register for the tickets—they are by no stretch of the imagination guaranteed tickets. Generously enough, however, this deposit will be refunded if the individual does not get tickets. Students are fortunate that there is not a processing fee.

Now $25 may not be much to the financially able members of the Wolfpack Club, but it is quite a hefty sum to a student who is attempting to live day to day and make ends meet. A $25 fee, with no tangible results for weeks, is not really sporting.

Perhaps there should be a similar lottery for Wolfpack Club members, and Wolfpack Club members alone—not their friends, families, and business associates—allowing them one ticket apiece. Would they favor such a system? The answer is fairly obvious. Maybe then they would realize the shortcomings of the system.

Certainly, the Wolfpack Club has done a lot for athletics at State, but should the students always be disregarded in favor of what's best for the club? We think not. But not being as powerful financially (and money talks), all we can do is continue to point out the inequities.

Since no drinking was allowed in Reynolds Coliseum unless authorized by the chancellor; the son of the head basketball coach was selected as head manager for the basketball team because he was more qualified; and students who wanted to purchase a ticket to the 1974 ACC basketball tournament had to fork over $25 just to be in a ticket lottery, thank goodness the official 1973–74 basketball season opened December 5 against East Carolina in Reynolds Coliseum.

Coach Sloan was playing the first game somewhat close to the vest. "The ECU-State series each year becomes more important and difficult," the coach was quoted in a pre-game. "The contest is not quite like a conference game, but it is becoming more parallel to it all the time. East Carolina played well against the (Duke) Blue Devils (before losing 82–69 four days earlier). With a couple of breaks, they could have won the game. In preparing for the ECU game, I want to stress the importance of our defensive play. It will play a major role in the ball game."

Chapter 11

After slow start, Wolfpack sinks Bucs

Reprinted from the Technician, December 7, 1973

By Ray Deltz

Staff Writer

For more than half of State's contest against East Carolina Wednesday night, it appeared that the Pirates basketball team was able to atone for a bit of the football team's humiliating defeat in Carter Stadium last September. But the strength of the nationally second-ranked Wolfpack became apparent in the second half as State glided to a 79–47 win.

Only when State began to show some heads-up play early in the second half did the Pack's lead begin to become somewhat comfortable. Throughout much of the first half, both teams consistently made turnovers, which kept the Wolfpack's lead from ever truly extending. Well into the first half, the lead changed hands several times before the Pack pulled away to their biggest lead of the half, 38–31, as the first half ended.

"We weren't ready to play in the first half," commented Wolfpack coach Norm Sloan. "They whipped us on the boards in the first half and even early in the second half."

Late in the first half, East Carolina employed somewhat of a semi-stall, which kept the Pirates in the ball game and prevented nervous Wolfpack fans from leaving their seats until the half was over.

Until Tom Burleson hit two foul shots at the 18:30 mark in the second half, it appeared the game would resemble a closely contested ACC battle. Finally, the Pack demonstrated to the near capacity coliseum crowd that the Wolfpack was indeed at least the number two team in the nation.

After the first 5½ minutes of the second half, the Wolfpack outhustled and outscored East Carolina by a 14–1 count and upped their lead to 52–35. And after 10 minutes of play in the second half, an unhealthy 38–31 halftime lead had turned into a 64–35 Wolfpack runaway.

Sloan felt State's national rankings were somewhat responsible for ECU's respectable play. "We are just going to have to adjust to the fact that since we are ranked high, every team we play will really be up for us," said Sloan.

In the final outcome, State's all-around team play in the second half, aided by East Carolina's poor touch from the field (27% in the second half), put the Wolfpack one game closer to the college basketball game of the year—with UCLA, of course. Only tonight's opponent, Yankee Conference representative Vermont, stands in the way of the Pack.

Chapter 12

Bruins get chance to stop Thompson

Reprinted from the Technician, December 7, 1973

After Wednesday night's basketball game, East Carolina head coach Tom Quinn said "State must move further toward the West Coast until they find a team that can play good defense against (David) Thompson and (Tom) Burleson." He was no doubt referring to the famed UCLA Bruins, who will get their chance to play defense against State a week from tomorrow in St. Louis on national TV.

Wolfpack fans have been looking forward to the dream game since last March when State didn't get a chance to test the Bruins in the NCAA championships because of probation. It's probably been the most talked about game in quite a while. Tickets for the game went like hotcakes.

While the fans are definitely thinking about the game, State coach Norman Sloan says he has not thought much about the game as yet. It's a good bet he and the players will be doing a lot of thinking next week about what he calls State's "13th most important game of the year."

As everyone knows, the Bruins are led by the big redhead Bill Walton, the college player of the year two straight seasons. But Walton is not the only UCLA player that can cause the opposition trouble.

61

Smooth Keith Wilkes operates at the high post and is a deadly shooter. Dave Meyers, a 6'8" junior, handles one wing spot, while Greg Lee, who played the point position last year is at the other wing. Tommy Curtis, a deft ball handler, operates at the point.

Both Sloan and UCLA's John Wooden assert this game should not be viewed as the 1973 championship since the personnel are not exactly the same (both teams lost two starters), and this is a new season.

Chapter 13

Christmas break: five wins, one loss

With the *Technician* suspending publication as usual after the December 7 edition for the semester break, there were no timely game stories for 6 games, which included the highly anticipated yet thoroughly disappointing game with UCLA.

The Bruins, the defending champion from the previous season, and State, the second ranked team at the end of the 1972–73 season, met in St. Louis with UCLA dominating the second half to defeat the Wolfpack, 84–66. State lead 33–32 at the half. Thompson paced State with 17 points. Towe had 14, and Burleson, with a game-high 15 rebounds, had 11 points. But the outcome was disappointing.

The loss dropped State from second in the national rankings to fifth.

Eight days prior to playing UCLA, State's warm-up for the Bruins was a demolishing of Vermont, 97–42 at home. Sixteen dressed-out State players played in the game, none for less than 4 minutes. No one played more than Thompson, who scored a game-high 19 points in 29 minutes. He also had 10 rebounds; Burleson had 11 rebounds. Phil Spence came off the bench to score 14 points and pull in 6 rebounds in 15 minutes. The Wolfpack led 41–14 at the half and outscored Vermont by double, 56–28 in the second period. State shot nearly 53% from the floor and held the opponent to just below 29%.

After the UCLA loss, the Wolfpack returned home and took out its frustrations on Georgia, defeating the Bulldogs, 94–60. This was another mismatch. Thompson's 28 points led all scorers and his 11 rebounds were tops for the game. Burleson had 15 points and 10 rebounds. Spence, coming off the bench and playing 29 minutes, had 11 points and 15 rebounds. State led 43–27 and the half.

In the Sugar Bowl tournament in New Orleans in late December, State knocked off Villanova, 97–82 and 18th-ranked Memphis State, 98–83. Against Villanova, Thompson hit 12 of 19 field goals to score a game-high 26 points. Burleson, 7 of 10 from the floor and 6 of 8 from the free throw line, had 20 points and pulled in a game-high 12 rebounds. Against Memphis, Thompson had 34 points and 11 rebounds; Burleson had 20 points and 15 rebounds.

Then, in the Big Four tournament in Greensboro in early January, the Pack defeated 4th-ranked North Carolina, 78–77 and Wake Forest, 91–73. Against North Carolina, the Wolfpack trailed 42–39 at the half. The Tar Heels made over 54% of its floor shots for the game while State was just below 50%. State's rebounding effort was instrumental against North Carolina as the Wolfpack dominated the boards, 40–22. Burleson had 22 points and 14 rebounds; Thompson had 20 points, 7 rebounds, and 7 assists. The Wolfpack's frustrations against North Carolina one night were taken out on Wake Forest in the first half the next night. State outscored the Deacons 51–33 in the first 20 minutes. State made over 54% of its field goal tries with Burleson leading the team with 23 points in 30 minutes of play. Thompson had 20 points, and Morris Rivers added 17 points.

Even with those 5 wins after the UCLA game, thoughts of the loss to the Bruins still lingered. Ken Lloyd, the then former sports editor, covered the game with UCLA and summarized the other games.

Chapter 14

Pack rebounds from UCLA loss

Reprinted from the Technician, January 9, 1974

By Ken Lloyd

Associate Sports Editor

Some called it the "Dream Game" while others referred to it as the "Game of the Decade." But for State's basketball Wolfpack, the much awaited contest with the mighty UCLA Bruins resembled more of a nightmare.

Even with Bill Walton, called by many the greatest collegiate player ever, sitting on the bench for half the game, the Bruins erased all doubts about them being true national champions by whipping the Wolfpack 84–66 in St. Louis before a national television audience on December 15.

But after the contest, State coach Norm Sloan shrugged off the loss and said it was "nothing bad for NC State. We've got to put it together now and be ready for our conference games."

The Wolfpack certainly has made inroads in getting ready for those conference games, which start this weekend, by winning two tournament championships and beating two nationally ranked squads in the process. First of all, two weeks after the disaster in St. Louis, State rebounded to win the Sugar Bowl basketball tourney in New Orleans by downing Memphis State.

Then last weekend, the Wolfpack showed more progress in winning the annual Big Four tournament in Greensboro, State's third such championship in the four-year history of the event. Even though State demolished a surprising Wake Forest in the championship game, the big win for the Wolfpack came in the first night against Carolina. State, which had fallen to fifth in the polls, moved up a notch by slipping past the fourth-ranked Tar Heels 78–77 in a real thriller. While Sloan said he thought his team would "still play better," the win went a long way in restoring some lost confidence.

Since the UCLA loss, State has been playing like a team with a special incentive. The Pack wants to regain their pride and wants another shot at the Bruins come March and the NCAA finals in Greensboro.

David Thompson, who could hit but 7 of 20 shots against the Bruins, said after the Big Four tourney that the UCLA game "took a little bit of our pride away from us, and we're trying to gain it back."

Going into the St. Louis encounter, the Wolfpack was admittedly a little cocky and overly confident, which could well be expected from a team that had won 29 straight games. But the loss to John Wooden's troops could be a blessing in disguise as far as the road to a possible national championship is concerned. The Bruins stunned the Pack and brought them back to earth.

"We blew an opportunity out there (in St. Louis)," said Monte Towe, State's little guard, who made 7 of 9 shots in the game. "But it might have been what we needed. We had been taking things for granted."

Being the first real test since the UCLA defeat, the Sugar Bowl tourney was crucial for State. The Wolfpack rose to the occasion, though, and came through with flying colors in winning the championship. "I could not have been more pleased with our performance in the Sugar Bowl tournament," said Sloan afterwards.

"We went into it lacking in some areas, but we came out with confidence."

Next, it was on to Greensboro for the Big Four. After blowing a 9-point lead Friday night, State hung on for a 1-point win over the Heels. State's defense and strong play on the backboards keyed the victory, which saw strong performances from several State players. Carolina coach Dean Smith said center Tommy Burleson was "just sensational" and played the best game of his career. Junior college transfers Phil Spence and Moe Rivers came into their own during the weekend.

Chapter 15

Preparing for the start of ACC games

Clemson was first on the Wolfpack's ACC schedule, Saturday, January 12. The day after the noon tip-off against the Tigers, the Wolfpack hosted Maryland, also a noon start, in Reynolds Coliseum. It was "Super Sunday" with the game against the Terrapins just prior to the NFL's Super Bowl game between the Miami Dolphins and the Minnesota Vikings.

Prior to the games with Clemson and Maryland, Coach Sloan said: "(I'm) very concerned about the Clemson game. They have potentially a very fine team. (Wayne) Rollins has put together outstanding games on several occasions this year, and even though he hasn't had a good overall game, he has shown flashes of what he is capable of doing. Tommy (Burleson) is going to be tremendously tested against Rollins. (Maryland has) every motivation in the world for this game. We upset them in their place a year ago on national TV, then won another game from them in Reynolds Coliseum, and then won a close one in the championship game of the ACC tournament."

With the back-to-back, day-to-day home games ahead, Ken Lloyd, associate sports editor, was concerned about crowd control—the booing and abusive type—in Reynolds Coliseum. Technician editorial writers zeroed in on crowd control—the ineffective smoking ban type—in Reynolds Coliseum. The Wolfpack basketball team was just trying to control its own destiny in games against Clemson and Maryland.

Chapter 16

SIDELINES: Crowd Control

Reprinted from the Technician, January 11, 1974

By Ken Lloyd

Associate Sports Editor

Crowd control at collegiate basketball games is becoming a serious problem all around the country. And in the Atlantic Coast Conference, where rivalries are so intense, the problem has grown immensely to the point where coaches and officials are having to make pleas to fans to control their fervor.

Reynolds Coliseum crowds have long had the reputation for their enthusiastic support for the Wolfpack, resulting in anything but a haven for visiting teams. But in the past few seasons, the treatment of the visitors to State has been insulting. Granted, the atmosphere at State is not worse than at any other arenas around the conference, but it is certainly no better.

With the ACC so strong this year from top to bottom, competition on the floor is bound to be fierce in just about every conference matchup. However, this will also breed more hatred among fans if they do not take stock and take a long, hard look at their actions.

Bad conduct at basketball games can do nothing but hurt the reputation of a university. With this Sunday's game with Lefty

Driesell's Maryland Terps on national television, the conduct of the State faithful will be put in the showcase for all the nation to see. Conduct such as on occasions in the past could very well damage State's good name.

In the past, treatment of visiting teams, particularly Carolina and Maryland, has been disgusting. The players and coaches have been subjected to verbal abuse and obscene gestures that seem to be only characteristic in basketball arenas. When people get inside a coliseum, they seem to lose all track of their senses and irrationality takes over.

One particularly frightful practice is the rushing onto the court by fans after a big victory. At last year's Carolina game, State fans exploded onto the court to rally around the winning Wolfpack, with pushing and shoving evident. In their zeal, they also made it difficult for the Tar Heel players to get off the court by running into them. Tempers became heated, and one dejected Carolina player started swinging at anybody close to him. Nothing serious developed, but it very easily could have, and indeed may occur in the future if the practice continues.

Whether fans realize it or not, disrespectful behavior often times acts just opposite of what they hope for it. State coach Norm Sloan says nothing fires him or his team up more than to get the full treatment at road games. No basketball team, even a fine one like State's, needs the opposition fired-up by the home fans.

To make Reynolds Coliseum a better place in which to view basketball games, it is going to take a concerted effort by all concerned—coaches, players, cheerleaders, students, and Wolfpackers.

Sloan, who has been a fiery sort on the bench in the past, says he is going to try to control himself this season so not to incite fans. He also talked to his players about their actions, both on the court and on the bench. The conduct of players has much to do with the disposition of the crowd.

In the past, cheerleaders have been the instigators of some of the bad behavior on the part of the fans because of bad cheers or the bad timing of cheers. Cheerleaders have the capacity to do much in the way of crowd control, but they have been lacking in this area in the past.

While the fans in the stands bear the major responsibility of controlling their behavior, they cannot be expected to do so if the coaches, players, and cheerleaders do not set a good example.

Students, State's most ardent supporters, are many times overzealous in their reactions to hated opponents. Students have their own rude cheers for which only they are responsible.

However, all the poor behavior has not come from the student sections. Much of the debris, as well as verbal abuse hurled at times to the floor, originates from the upstairs area where the season ticket holders sit.

While there needs to be better treatment of visiting teams, this does not mean the support for the Wolfpack has to be decreased. Some of the energy used to degrade opponents can be used to build the Pack.

So, this weekend, let's make Reynolds Coliseum the model for the rest of the conference. Greet Maryland and Clemson with polite applause, or better yet, just ignore them. Instead, yell like hell for the Pack. The Terps and the Tigers won't know what's happening.

Chapter 17

Coliseum smoking ban ineffective

Editorial reprinted from the Technician, January 14, 1974

Crowd control at Reynolds Coliseum still has a long way to go. At Sunday's Maryland-State contest, the Coliseum was filled with smoke even though there is a ban on smoking in the Coliseum. Little or no action was taken against the offenders, and as long as this permissive attitude is taken by Coliseum authorities, the situation will not improve.

The only mention of the ban was made by the announcer, and then, it was made only once prior to the start of the game. People who break rules have notoriously short memories, and many of them chose to ignore the announcement as the game wore on. By the second half, the reaches of Reynolds Coliseum were once again filled with choking smoke.

As with all other individual decisions, a person has the *right* to smoke. But this right is only operative as long as it does not infringe upon the rights of others. Few people could seriously claim that smoking within a confined area, such as Reynolds Coliseum, is inoffensive to those sitting around them. Many people are allergic to smoke or are unable to breathe smoke-filled air comfortably.

But there are more serious effects to be taken into consideration. It has been proven scientifically that people who do not smoke but who breathe smoked-filled air suffer the same consequences as to those who smoke. The quantities of smoke filling the air and being inhaled by non-smokers are detrimental to them as well. Smoke is dangerous and cancer causing whether it is inhaled directly or indirectly. It is a definite hazard either way.

Unfortunately, many smokers have become such slaves to the habit that they find it hard to refrain from it even for the space of approximately two hours that it takes to conduct a basketball game. It would be better if they did not even show up for the game if they have such little willpower. No doubt they enjoy smoking immensely, but there are probably many more people who wish that they would abstain.

The Coliseum authorities are only paying lip service to the great majority of the fans by making announcements about the smoking ban without taking action to enforce this supposed ban. As in many areas, examples have to be made before the ban can become effective. As long as people can continue to smoke without being rebuked, they will continue to smoke to the great discomfort of many of those around them.

Coliseum authorities should redirect their efforts, informing both fans and security officers that smoking is prohibited, but moreover, escorting those who continue to ignore the prohibition from the Coliseum. Smoking is dangerous and causes great discomfort to large numbers of fans. It is a serious business and should be dealt with seriously and vigorously.

Chapter 18

David Thompson dunks Terps

From the Technician, January 14, 1974

By Jim Pomeranz

Sports Editor

State's Wolfpack came out growling Sunday afternoon in Reynolds Coliseum and whipped a well-disciplined Maryland team before a sellout crowd and a national television audience, 80–74.

At times, State looked unconquerable as they built leads up to 14 points while at other times, Maryland, behind the hot hands of senior forward Tom McMillan and sophomore guard John Lucas, pulled ahead of the Pack by one point. McMillan and Lucas each scored 24 points.

A slick forward by the name of David Thompson was the story for the Wolfpack. The 6'4" junior, who leaps as if he were 6'10", tossed in 41 points and pulled down 8 rebounds.

Once, however, the All-American's extraordinary leaping ability (42 inches straight up off the floor) had a damper put on it. A pass to Thompson high over the goal was caught and carefully dropped in for 2 points, only to have offensive goal tending called, nullifying the basket.

"David's play was so beautiful," State head coach Norm Sloan commented after the game. "I knew the call would come sometime during the season. Not allowing the dunk takes the thrill out of college basketball."

State's lead fluctuated through the game until midway through the second half when the Wolfpack had built a 14-point lead and the Terrapin offense began to pluck away at it.

From the 10:07 mark in the final period until the final buzzer, Maryland outscored the Pack 20–14. During that time, Lucas hit 12 points for Maryland and Thompson hit 8 points for State, two of which Sloan said were crucial. Those two State points came with only 53 seconds remaining in the game and put the Wolfpack ahead, 80–74. Neither team was able to put any other scoring into the record book.

With about 5 minutes remaining in the game after a State timeout, the Wolfpack became very deliberate handling the ball. State led 76–70 at that point, but 2½ minutes later, the Wolfpack had committed two turnovers and Maryland had turned them into points and cut the State lead to only 2 points.

State 7'4" center Tommy Burleson then hit two crucial free throws to put the Pack ahead by 4 again, and 1 minute later, Thompson hit that shot to set the final score.

After the game, Sloan was questioned about the slow-down effort of the Wolfpack.

"Anytime there is a tempo change, there is a question of what happens," said Sloan. "We did not go to our tease offense until under 1 minute remained. Before then, we were just handling the ball. They (Maryland) were still in their zone press, and we wanted good ball handling. Our tease was good," he concluded.

After the game, State guard Monte Towe explained the slowdown in the last 5 minutes.

"Coach Sloan didn't say a word about it," the little man said. "I looked at David (Thompson), and David looked at me and the rest of the guys, and we just went into it."

In the first 3 minutes of play, State hurriedly rolled up a 7-point lead, 13–6, only to see that vanish in the next 5 minutes and to fall behind, 21–22. But the Pack stormed right back and took control for the remainder of the initial period and led at the half, 45–41.

During those first 3 minutes, it was the shooting of Thompson that gave the Pack its lead as he hit for 7 of State's 13 points. And it was Thompson again that led the Pack to the halftime lead as he scored a total of 23 points for the first half.

As the second half opened up, the Terrapins opened up and took control of the game for the first 4 minutes, outscoring the Pack 9–4, leading 50–49.

But the Pack began to wake up, and Maryland quit hitting the basket as State could not miss for the next 6 minutes and outscored the Terrapins 19–4 for their biggest lead of the game, 68–54.

Scoring behind Thompson for State was Burleson, with 13 points and 10 rebounds, and small guard Monte Towe, with 12 points. On Saturday, Towe had scored 19 points to lead the Wolfpack to victory over conference foe Clemson, 96–68.

After that game with the Tigers, Sloan had said that the State defense "is getting better and better every game." And the Wolfpack proved they were improving as they created 20 turnovers of Maryland and stole the ball 8 times away from the usually selfish Terps.

Completing the scoring for State was Moe Rivers, with 6 points, and Phil Spence and Tim Stoddard, with 4 each. Len Elmore had 13 points for the Terps, and Maurice Howard added 11.

Chapter 19

Sloan: 'You have to win the big ones and we did'

From the Technician, January 14, 1974

By Bill Moss

Staff Writer

"It was a great win we had to have," said a happy Wolfpack coach Norm Sloan after his charges had defeated Maryland, 80–74. "You have to win the big ones, and we did."

Win the big one was exactly what the Wolfpack did yesterday at Reynolds Coliseum. David Thompson foiled every defense Maryland coach Lefty Driesell could think of as he teased the twines for 41 points on 14 of 20 field goals and 13 free throws.

"David played fantastic," Sloan understated. "He is a great player," he continued, saying the very obvious.

"Monte (Towe) and (Moe) Rivers were good, and (Tim) Stoddard came through like a champion," he praised.

Indeed, State's two guards, Towe and Rivers, ran around and under the Terrapin defense until (the Terps) they were dizzy. Towe scored 12 points, mostly on 25 footers, and directed the State offense like a field general.

"I didn't say anything, but I thought about the UCLA game," said the miniature guard. "We just couldn't lose twice on national TV. The ACC is the best there is, and we tried to show that."

And a typical ACC it was. Driesell was understandably disheartened after the loss, but he made few excuses. "There was that one little spurt when we lost that discipline on offense, and we had people in foul trouble," Lefty murmured. "The charging fouls were totally ridiculous. We had 6 or 7 in the first half."

Maryland, playing only 6 or 7 players a game, got in deep trouble early, and the fouls were what really hurt in the end.

Fouls and David Thompson.

"We played him (Thompson) man for man and wanted to make him shoot from the outside, but he hit 'em outside," Lefty said in a manner that indicated that any defense is futile.

Three players tried to guard the 6'4" phenomenon, and three failed miserably. They even tried fouling, but Thompson hit on 13 of 17 attempts at the charity stripe in addition to pulling down 8 rebounds.

In the final analysis, the Maryland game was decided by Towe's floor leadership, (Tommy) Burleson's more than competent play against Len Elmore, and one David Thompson who was super on Sunday.

Chapter 20

Euphoria turns sour

The day after State's wins over Maryland and Clemson, the campus was buzzing with excitement, but events of that Monday tempered the excitement. Two athletes had been arrested.

Chapter 21

State athletes cited in arrests

Reprinted from the Technician, January 16, 1974

By Jim Pomeranz

Sports editor

State basketball player Morris Rivers and Allen Scott, a diver on the swimming team, were arrested in separate incidents Monday.

Rivers was arrested late Monday night at the Mission Valley Convenient Food Mart on the charge of misdemeanor larceny. It was reported that he had shoplifted a $.37 box of Anacin.

According to Richard E. Elsener of the Merchants Detective Agency, Rivers entered the store at approximately 10:15 p.m. "He fiddled for a few minutes between the drug counter and the checkout counter," said Elsener. "He then reached into his pocket, pulled out some change, and looked at it. After putting the change back, he picked up one box of Anacin or aspirin and while examining it, dropped it on the floor. After replacing the box, he picked up another box and put it in his pocket while the girl at the checkout counter was not looking."

Elsener said that after Rivers had left the store and was sitting in his car, Elsener approached him, asked Rivers to remove himself from the car, and hand over the box he had taken from the store.

Elsener commented that Rivers had offered to pay for the Anacin once back inside the store. The detective continued to say that Rivers "put up no resistance. He explained," said Elsener, "that he had gone to his car to get money from his girl to pay for the Anacin."

Raleigh police officer R.N. Hogg, the arresting officer, said that Rivers "claimed he told the clerk he would be right back" because "he was going to the car to get some change." Hogg also stated that Rivers had said the clerk "evidently didn't hear him."

Coach Norm Sloan said Tuesday that he had not "gone far enough into the case to make any other decision" other than suspending Rivers for "violation of curfew." The suspension is for only one game (Virginia). According to Sloan, Rivers will not be allowed to practice with or make the trip to Virginia with the squad.

Curfew for State basketball players varies from week to week, and, according to Sloan, 11:30 p.m. was this week's limit. Sloan said the only reason Rivers had missed his curfew was that he "was trying to clear up the matter." Sloan did comment that Rivers' side of the story and the report filed with the police "conflict."

The junior guard was released after a $100 bond was posted. His trial is set for February 14 at 9 a.m. in Wake District Court.

Rivers could not be reached for comment.

Early Monday morning state and local law enforcement agencies arrested State student athlete Allen Scott on two counts of possession and distribution of marijuana. Scott is a diver on the nationally ranked State swimming team.

Almost two years ago, Scott was arrested on possession of marijuana. He was suspended from the swimming team for one year but allowed to keep his scholarship aid.

Swimming coach Don Easterling said the matter was one for diving coach John Candler to decide, but continued to say that "if it's his second offense, and he is found guilty, then as far as I'm concerned, he will not be a member of the swimming team."

Candler said he had not investigated the case enough to make a decision at this time.

Chapter 22

Athletes in action?

Editorial reprinted from the Technician, January 16, 1974

Once again, State athletes have found themselves in trouble with the law. In the past few years, it has become almost commonplace to read about Wolfpack athletes being caught with their hands in the cookie jar. Now, basketball player Morris Rivers and diver Allen Scott have both been charged with law violations. These newest occurrences, together with those that have taken place in the past, reflect badly on State's athletic programs, but more than this, they reflect badly on the university as a whole.

It waits to be seen what kind of action will be taken against Rivers and Scott. Certainly some legal action will be initiated as is customary if the two are proven guilty. However, it is uncertain what measures, if any, will be taken against them by the university or the athletic department. Rivers has so far been suspended from the Virginia game for breaking curfew. Of course, if Scott is found guilty as charged, it will be his second violation for possession of marijuana, and the penalties of the law will probably make university action unnecessary.

It will be interesting to note how students react to this latest news. In the past, athletes who have violated the law have become something of celebrities on campus. Students have been slow to respond to the seriousness of the unlawful offenses committed.

Perhaps because the violators were athletes, they were treated somewhat differently in the minds of the students. The students follow winning teams and want winning teams, and often they are willing to overlook such violations in order that the winning tradition may be kept up. Just as many students are reluctant to report fellow students who cheat in class, they are also reluctant to see anything wrong when athletes who participate on winning teams are charged with crimes.

Since a lot of athletes are getting a "free ride" through school due to their scholarships, they have certain obligations to the university to remain above reproach. The focus of the public is zeroed in on them much more than on the individual, unexceptional student. Therefore, the public draws a lot of conclusions about the university as a whole from the actions of athletes. Whether they like it or not, this is how it works. Hopefully, Rivers and Scott are innocent of the charges leveled against them. Their innocence would reflect well on both the athletes and the university. But, if they are guilty, the university should take definite and fitting action against them in order to absolve itself of complicity in harboring law-breakers within its athletic department.

Chapter 23

Rivers out; Pack back up

With Morris Rivers serving a one-game suspension, the Wolfpack prepared to travel to Virginia. The suspension was the only rule the team had as a result of a meeting between Monte Towe and coach Norm Sloan in December. After the UCLA game, Towe thought the team needed a little more discipline. Sloan asked Towe what he had in mind, reminding Towe that if rules were broken, there needed to be consequences. So, Towe suggested the curfew rule, which was put into place that day. So, about a month later, Rivers broke curfew and had to sit out the Virginia game. The arrest and allegation of stealing a $.37 tin of aspirin was not a team rules violation.

There was no mention of Rivers in the pre-Virginia game, but Sloan did emphasize the importance of the game at the Cavaliers. "The Virginia games are always tough games for us, and this one will be particularly difficult since Virginia will be at home." Sloan was quoted in the story by staff writer Steve Baker. "We've just come off a demanding weekend, but luckily, we were victorious, and I feel this has helped us. We seem to be getting more cohesion on our defense. We're forcing the action, causing more turnovers, and giving the opposition more problems."

While the Wolfpack's loss to UCLA dropped State from second to fifth in the national polls, the 7-game winning streak, especially the wins against North Carolina and Maryland, pushed State up to the third spot.

The *Technician* was published most Mondays, Wednesdays, and Fridays, and with early deadlines, it was nearly impossible for results from Tuesday and Thursday games to make the next day's edition. It was not unusual for game stories to skip an issue while game reviews were mixed in between, for instance, when State played at Virginia on Thursday, January 17, and then hosted UNC-Charlotte on Saturday, January 19. After that, there was a Tuesday, January 22 date at Carolina.

Chapter 24

Covering SPORTS: The slowdown

Reprinted from the Technician, January 18, 1974

By Jim Pomeranz

Sports Editor

Last year before Carolina's basketball game with Miami (Ohio), the *Daily Tar Heel* wrote that the Redskins would be a needed break in the tough Tar Heel schedule. It went on to say that a Carolina victory would not fail to develop.

The next issue of the DTH apologized for the article because the Tar Heels were soundly defeated by the Miami team.

Tomorrow night, State's basketball team will be confronted with a similar situation. The University of North Carolina at Charlotte basketball team will invade Reynolds Coliseum Saturday night at 8 p.m. in what has been termed by UNC-C supporters, coaches, and players as *the game*. The 49ers schedule for the past few years has been filled with some of the nation's top twenty teams in hopes of gaining national recognition for the school's athletic program.

State started a series with the Charlotte school last season and defeated the 49ers, 100–64.

Some people are taking the game lightly; however, State head coach Norm Sloan talks differently. He says that UNC-C is looking for a highly ranked team to knock off, and State would be that team.

Robert Earl Blue, last season's top scorer for UNC-C, will be the main scoring threat against the number three nationally ranked Wolfpack.

Prior to the Virginia game last night, State All-American Dave Thompson led all Wolfpack and ACC scorers with 24.9 scoring clip. Center Tom Burleson is averaging 15.1 points per game and is pulling down an average of 11.5 rebounds for each contest.

*   *   *   *

Last Sunday against Maryland, the Wolfpack basketball team received an undesirable amount of booing from the fans when late in the game, a spread type offense was being played by State. State had built up a 14-point lead earlier in the game by running with the Terrapins, and even though Maryland had pulled within 6 points, many observers felt that the spread offense was unnecessary and that the booing was justified.

Norm Sloan's charges have attempted such an offense, named the "tease" offense, in previous games, and in those games, the opposing team was able to create turnovers and gain a few points on the Pack. Maryland pulled to within 2 points while State held the ball.

State is fortunate to have one of the fastest, if not THE fastest, basketball team in the nation, and such offensive patterns should not be needed in the Wolfpack game plan.

However, it has been added to the Wolfpack attack. Coach Norm Sloan explains the system is used to create a one-on-one matchup, and when successful, this has been the case.

This reporter was at first angered with the slowdown. The reason is that what got you there seems to be the best thing to finish with. So, if fast breaking is what has made the team win, why the change?

89

But the success of the Wolfpack throughout the years has not only been because of the caliber of the players. Much credit is due to the coach of the team.

Norman Sloan came to State as head coach in May of 1966 after Press Maravich had vacated the top spot for a similar position at LSU. While at State, the fiery coach has produced 5 winning seasons on his way to compiling an overall 117–70 record, including on undefeated season and 2 ACC titles.

In two particular cases, there were outstanding games played by the Pack in slowdown contests. In the 1968 ACC tournament, State faced what was then a very good and highly ranked Duke basketball team and beat them, 12–10. In the same tournament in 1970, State held the ball against a tough South Carolina squad and beat them, 42–39, in a double overtime game.

The slowdown by no means is what is always best for the Pack. Only when the odds are overwhelmingly against State, as in the above cases, should such tactics be used.

As for the booing in Reynolds last Sunday, that just happened to be the reaction of many fans who paid to see what they term as a "contest with action." Many fans do not like the idea of the third ranked team in the nation using slowdown tactics to win ball games.

However, that tactic has been used by a sister institution of the Wolfpack, and that school's fans have always met the situation with applause. I speak of the famed four-corner offense used by Carolina. Dean Smith, the Tar Heel coach, has been highly successful with such an offense at the Chapel Hill school and has rarely received criticism for using it. When unfavorable remarks are used, they come from opposing supporters.

Sloan is the coach of the Wolfpack and has turned a basketball program that had declined from national prominence into one of the nation's best.

Chapter 25

Burleson leads State past Cavs, 49ers

Reprinted from the Technician, January 21, 1974

By Steve Baker

Staff Writer

For all of you "Tom Terrific" fans who have cut classes to see his adventures on Captain Kangaroo each morning, good news! Tom has left the captain to join the Wolfpack, and you can now see him in person in Reynolds Coliseum.

Tom Terrific has grown from the little boy who used to fight evil with the aid of his wonder dog into 7'4" Tommy Burleson, who now battles his opponents with the aid of a pack of wolves.

Last Thursday, *The Cavalier Daily*, the University of Virginia student newspaper, made the mistake of calling Burleson "Timid Tom." Burleson took his revenge by dominating the helpless Cavalier cagers, then carried his fired-up play over into the game Saturday night against UNC-Charlotte. Behind Burleson's 29 points and 10 rebounds, the Pack bombed the 49ers, 104–72.

Perhaps the UVA newspaper had judged Burleson on his shooting percentage in the Wolfpack victory over Maryland the Sunday prior to the Virginia game. In that contest Burleson hit only 3 of 9 shots from the floor. Shooting percentage is a poor way to judge an athlete, however, and Burleson has proved that fact.

91

"The Maryland game was the poorest shooting game I've had in a long time. The ball just wouldn't fall for me. Overall though, I feel I played a pretty good game," commented Burleson after the Pack had defeated UNC-C.

Since Maryland, Burleson's shooting has been near perfect and that, combined with the rest of the Pack's play, has led to two decisive victories over Virginia, 90–70, and UNC-C. Against Virginia, Burleson canned 22 points and hauled down 13 rebounds.

"I don't think my play has been that much different," stated Burleson. "The ball's just starting to drop for me more."

State head coach Norman Sloan sees Burleson's progress in much the same way. "I thought Tommy played a fine game against Maryland. His shots just wouldn't fall. Against Virginia and UNC-C, they did."

Burleson has had plenty of help in State's last two outings. David Thompson was up to his usual antics in the Virginia game, dropping 30 points. Monte Towe also had a fine night, contributing 20 points. Towe and guard Mark Moeller, making his first start for the Wolfpack, paced the Pack to an 11–0 lead and kept the Cavaliers from getting their game plan rolling in the early going.

UNC-C came into Reynolds Coliseum with a 10–2 record and high hopes of upsetting the 3rd-ranked Wolfpack. The upset was not to be, however. From the start, State took command and continued to keep control throughout the contest. It wasn't, however, one of the Wolfpack's better games, and Sloan pointed this out. "We played very ragged. We had good periods, average periods, and mediocre periods. It was much like some of our earlier games this season.

"UNC-C was fired up and came to play," continued the State mentor. "They came at us and never let up. I think they're better than last year, but I think we are too."

David Thompson, Morris Rivers, and Phil Spence were the three top men backing up Burleson's high-scoring performance. Thompson tossed in 16 points, Rivers contributed 16, and Spence 11.

Tuesday night, the Wolfpack meets Carolina in its 3rd conference test. Sloan doesn't feel that the big victory over UNC-C will make any decisive difference. "There was absolutely nothing gained or lost in our victory over UNC-C," stated Sloan after the nonconference victory. "The game with UNC-C and the one with Carolina will be two different types of basketball games altogether. UNC-C doesn't have the big guards or a big man who is also a good leaper like Bobby Jones."

Burleson was a teammate of Carolina's Jones and Mitch Kupchak this past summer in the World University Games and feels this is in some ways helpful. "I don't think it will help my game that much," stated Burleson. "It might help me prepare a little better. The good aspects of having played with Jones and Kupchak are the experience with and mutual respect we have for each other. It makes for good rivalry and competitiveness, and at the same time, it is less likely for tempers to flare since we are good friends."

Chapter 26

Striking a nerve; removing the sting

The arrest of and subsequent charges against basketball player Morris Rivers, struck a nerve with the campus basketball fans. One in particular, senior Ed Caram, also a *Technician* staff photographer, voiced his opinion is a January 21 letter to the editor:

> Recently the Technician reported the arrest of an NC State student for shoplifting. This particular incident involved a bottle of Anacin valued at 37 cents. The student told authorities that he had merely gone out to his car to get the correct amount of money from his girlfriend, and further, that he had told the clerk that he would be right back with the money. This incident occurred at the Mission Valley Convenient Food Mart, near campus, off Western Blvd.
>
> The student was apprehended by a store detective and turned over to Raleigh police for shoplifting. I understand that store owners have an investment to protect and that shoplifting is a real problem and a cause for higher prices at many stores. I also understand that many stores hire private detectives to protect their investments. I believe storeowners have every right to protect the money that they work hard to earn.

I believe that merchants also have a responsibility to apply a degree of reasonableness when one of their customers is apprehended for suspected shoplifting. Imagine how many arrests and trials there would be if every person who picked up a pack of gum or a 2-cent piece of candy and put it in his pocket so he could carry other packages was apprehended and sent downtown to jail because he forgot to pay when he got to the door.

Further, imagine how many people have gone to their car to ask someone who was riding with them to give them some money because they did not have the right change in their pocket. I know that I have told a cashier that I would be back in a minute, and that I was just going to get the right change. The fact is that anyone who went out could be arrested as a shoplifter if he wasn't given the chance to come back in.

The particular instance in which the NC State student was arrested for a 37-cent bottle of Anacin is questionable. Some item of greater value might be believable. If the operator of the Mission Valley Convenient Food Mart can't be more reasonable and understanding before he sends his customers to the police, then maybe his customers should question whether or not to buy things at his store.

On the day the Wolfpack took out UNC-Charlotte, UCLA was losing its first game of the year, 71–70, to Notre Dame, ending an 88-game winning streak. This loss took the sting out of the Wolfpack's loss to the Bruins in December. The day before State played at Carolina, the *Technician* editorial page took advantage of UCLA's loss to speak in favor of intercollegiate athletics. And, on the day before the State-Carolina basketball game, Bill Jackson, the voice of the Wolfpack football and basketball play-by-play for more than 20 years, passed away after a battle with cancer.

Chapter 27

Silver lining

Editorial reprinted from the Technician, January 21, 1974

Saturday, January 19, 1974, will go down in the annals of sports as one of the most historic days in collegiate competition. The University of California at Los Angeles, better known to the world at large as UCLA, experienced a major setback on the basketball court. After amassing an unbelievable 88-game winning streak, UCLA's basketball Bruins were defeated by Notre Dame by a score of 71–70. The Irish only led once in the game, at the end, but that was quite enough. Their slender victory epitomized the spirit and competition found in and engendered by collegiate sports.

The Irish were the last in a procession of nationally ranked number two teams, which had challenged the Bruins this season—the other notable members of this group being State and the University of Maryland, both finally defeated by UCLA. It was looking more and more like coach John Wooden was on his way to another undefeated season. But the young Notre Dame team threw a barricade in his path that the "Wizard of Westwood" did not foresee.

But the ballgame was much more than the end of an amazing win streak. It was a lesson in courage and faith by the underdog. Although the winning team trailed the majority of the game, many times by wide, seemingly insurmountable margins, they always rallied and brought themselves back into the ballgame.

All in all, the Notre Dame team and coaches and, perhaps most importantly, the spirit of the home-team fans brought about the unexpected coup. The combination of all of these factors helped to show once again the value of collegiate athletics.

Collegiate athletics does have an important place on any campus. It gives many disadvantaged young men the chance for a college education that they could not normally have. It brings in scholarship money for the schools and gains them much needed national recognition when it is successful. It exhibits the many benefits of physical education and good health.

Of course, athletics necessarily should always come as a second consideration behind academics. After all, colleges and universities have the primary responsibility of first educating those who enroll. But as long as competition is kept in its proper perspective, it can be good for the entire school, not just the athletes involved in the programs.

Athletic contests are illustrative of many aspects of life. There is triumph and disappointment in—as the American Broadcasting Company has so aptly termed it—"the thrill of victory and the agony of defeat." Successful athletic programs must necessarily go through many struggles to achieve the pinnacle.

There is undoubtedly much to be learned from sports. The student fans experience the same gloom or exaltation as do those on the playing floor. A catharsis of emotion is affected as if the fans were attending a theatrical production. It is also an educational experience in which people learn that losing is not always the end of the world.

Indeed, athletics should not be unduly condemned. Athletics is also a method of education, but more than that, many times, it is just plain fun.

Chapter 28

SIDELINES: When State and Carolina Meet

Reprinted from the Technician, January 21, 1974

By Ken Lloyd

Associate Sports Editor

When State and Carolina meet in anything, they need no introduction.

Just say the Wolfpack and Tar Heels will play at a certain time, and that will normally suffice. Fans know to expect a knock-down–drag-out affair, regardless of the teams' records.

But a basketball game between the two schools is a little different since usually one team, or both, is ranked very high in the nation. Plus, the rivalry is so intense between teams and fans, people expect a little more. A State-Carolina basketball game is something special, possibly created by some divine right.

The teams go at it once again tomorrow night at Carolina's "Blue Heaven." State is ranked third in the nation while Carolina is fifth, and both are undefeated in Atlantic Coast Conference play. But, like all these contests, even more is at stake—pride.

Since Norman Sloan came back to his alma mater in 1966, State has managed to win only one game in Chapel Hill with that one coming last season. But, after being drubbed by the Tar Heels repeatedly for a number of years, the Wolfpack has atoned for that somewhat by winning the last five meetings. State swept a trio of contests last season and took the first this season, a 72–71 squeaker in the Big Four Tournament a little over two weeks ago.

In that one, State blew a 9-point lead after going into a slowdown and had to hang on for dear life to salvage the victory. Carolina's Ed Stahl missed a shot that hit the rim in the final seconds.

Since the State encounter, the Tar Heels have had some close calls. The following Saturday, they weathered a furious rally by Virginia in defeating the Cavaliers, who pulled to within 3 points before Carolina stretched out the score.

Then last Saturday, Duke gave the Heels all they could ask for before succumbing 73–71 on some last-minute heroics by Bobby Jones. With 7 seconds left in the game, the smooth Jones adeptly intercepted a Blue Devil inbound pass and drove for the winning basket.

After that heart stopper, Tar Heel coach Dean Smith said, "I hope we have some shots left for Tuesday night." It's a good bet they will.

State, meanwhile, has looked awesome in recent games, particularly against Maryland and Virginia. Last Thursday night, the Pack swamped the Cavaliers in Charlottesville by the totally unexpected margin of 20 points.

Against the Cavaliers, State disdained its usual man-to-man defense in the second half in favor of a zone in order to get ready for the Tar Heels. With Carolina's good inside personnel and patented offensive patterns, State may have to go to a zone to neutralize the Heels. Their weave around the basket continually makes for easy buckets against man-to-man defenses underneath.

Thus, the stage is set for another Carolina-State matchup. Like all the rest, it should be something special—that is, until the next one.

Chapter 29

Covering SPORTS: State will miss Jackson

From the Technician, January 23, 1974

By Jim Pomeranz

Sports Editor

Bill Jackson, "the Voice of the Wolfpack" for the past 12 years, will be missed at State. The man who helped bring the excitement of State sports into the homes of many fans died early Monday morning at the age of 56.

Jackson, along with Wally Ausley, started broadcasting State sporting events in 1961 on the Wolfpack Sports Network through radio station WPTF.

This writer only met Jackson recently, but has always held a high respect for him. As a young follower of the Pack, I would always turn on the radio, and, without fail, I would hear the voice so familiar to many.

For many basketball games, I would sit by the radio and listen to the Voice of the Wolfpack. There were times that, even when the Pack was on television, I would turn down the sound on the set and turn on WPTF. It was always Bill Jackson I heard.

Football games were the same way. Saturday afternoons when I did not make the trip to Raleigh or when State was on the road, Bill Jackson was on the radio.

He always had a great knowledge of what was going on down on the court or on the field.

Many people remember Jackson for his early morning "BJ Show" on WPTF. That show was just as much part of the day as was waking up and eating breakfast. The BJ Show was plainly part of the morning routine.

And of course, there was "Gabfest." That show was a small part of the morning, but the conversation between Jackson and Ausley was a great show for the fun of it. I remember the continuous plugs for the Wolfpack.

Jackson and Ausley on those Wolfpack sports broadcasts made listening easy and fun. State sports will greatly miss Bill Jackson.

State assistant athletic director Frank Weedon has been around the two men probably as much as or more than anyone at State throughout the years. He said "they (Jackson and Ausley) and the Wolfpack Sports Network were always considered part of the team party wherever we went."

Weedon stated that while Jackson hosted the "BJ Show" on WPTF early in the morning, he always created "a lot of good publicity for the Wolfpack. He always talked about State athletics," commented Weedon late Monday afternoon.

"And then on Gabfest (a show with Jackson and Ausley), we would call the radio station up and get Bill and Wally to talk a little about State," commented the former State sports information director. "They would always help us sell tickets to events when we had extras. Bill would give us that little bit of publicity we needed other than advertising."

Weedon said that, recently, he and Jackson had been discussing State athletics as they were always doing, and Jackson had mentioned two Wolfpack games that he thought of the most.

"One was the State-Carolina football game in 1960," remarked Weedon. "State won it 3–0. There was an interception by State's Claude Gibson in the end zone to save a touchdown."

During that game, WPTF was broadcasting Carolina's game. It was the next year they started broadcasting State games.

The second game that Weedon said Jackson remembered so well was the State-Houston football contest in 1967. State won it 16–6 and made a big jump in the rankings that week due to the high ranking of Houston.

"At halftime, Fred Waring was directing a 2,000-member band along with a chorus," said Weedon. "They were playing patriotic music. I turned and looked at Bill, and there were tears coming down his face. He was really moved by the music."

Weedon said that Jackson "never let anything go uncovered" when covering a ball game. Jackson would always compile a thorough scouting report on the other team. Weedon said during football season this would mean starting work early in the week.

Weedon also said Jackson was a "lousy golfer but loved to play the game. He also loved to fish on the coast," added Weedon.

Jackson was named the North Carolina Annual Sportscaster of the Year in 1960, 1962, and 1968. He was the Sports Director of WPTF, and on November 1, 1972, he was named vice president and program manager of that radio station, which he first started working with in 1952.

During the fifties, he was part of a broadcast team with Jim Reid as they mostly covered Carolina sports.

Jackson was a contributor to the Fellowship of Christian Athletes. His love of State sports and the contributions he made to them gain him the Award of Merit in 1970 for distinguished service to the university by a non-alumnus. Jackson was also awarded a membership in the State Monogram Club.

Bill Jackson and the Wolfpack go hand in hand. He will definitely be missed by State fans from all over.

Chapter 30

SIDELINES: Thompson is State's franchise

From the Technician, January 25, 1974

By Ken Lloyd

Associate Sports Editor

In the short span of just 9 days, David Thompson has proven without a doubt that he's the franchise in basketball here at State.

Without him, State would probably be just another good team, good enough to battle for third place in the Atlantic Coast Conference. But with Thompson in the lineup and having a decent game, the Pack may very well be the best team in the nation.

It seems like the All-American from Shelby has taken it upon himself to personally demolish the top pretenders to the Wolfpack's ACC throne, Maryland and Carolina, both of whom are just a step behind State in the national rankings.

First of all, Thompson almost singlehandedly sent Lefty Driesell's Terps falling into defeat back on January 13 by scoring a career high 41 points. Then he came right back last Tuesday night to lead the Pack past fired-up Carolina, 83–80, in Chapel Hill.

In that one, Thompson did just about everything—scoring 26 points from inside, outside, and in between, hauling in 10 rebounds, blocking numerous shots, and generally dazzling the hyper crowd.

"Tonight it was a one man thing," lauded Carolina's Bobby Jones after the game. "Thompson is one of the greatest players I've ever seen. He just goes up and over you."

Jones, one of the finest defensive players in the nation, got the first crack at trying to stop Thompson and soon found it could be a harrowing experience.

"It's really frustrating trying to guard Thompson," he said. "When he goes up for that jump shot, all you can do is put a hand in his face and hope he misses."

Jones said no one man can stop Thompson and even two may have trouble. "Only he alone can neutralize himself."

Carolina has yet to beat a Thompson-led State team with the Pack winning the last 5 contests over these 2 seasons. "We can beat them with Thompson playing a good game, but not when he's awesome like he was tonight," said Jones. "It would help if he had a bad game.

"He will just not let them lose," added the senior from Charlotte. "When State needs something, Thompson gets it for them."

Carolina coach Dean Smith also marveled at Thompson's talent, especially on one tip where he went high above the rim ("5'," according to Smith), reached out and seemed to grab the ball and guide it toward the basket.

"Thompson showed tonight he is definitely, outside of (Bill) Walton, the most dominant in the game today," said the coach.

While Thompson makes State's team, the Wolfpack is far from a one-man team. And the Carolina game proved it.

Monte Towe ran the Tar Heels ragged with his ball-hawking. He ripped for 21 points as he bombed from way downtown with marksmanship precision. His ball handling gave Carolina problems all night. "With our pressure, Towe does a great job of handling the ball," said Smith.

Tom Burleson also played a dominant role, scoring 14 points and controlling the boards for 11 rebounds. "Tommy's a lot stronger than he was last year," said Jones. "And he has become a lot smarter player too."

Phil Spence added to the Wolfpack board strength by also pulling down 10 stray shots while also scoring 8 points. "Spence was a key to State's team tonight," noted Smith. "He got some big rebounds."

State seems to be getting a little revenge now for the agony suffered at the hands of the Tar Heels in the late 1960s and the early 1970s when Carolina won everything in sight. Between 1966 and 1970, Carolina won 10 straight from the Pack. But when the 2 teams meet again on February 26 in Reynolds Coliseum, State will be riding the crest of a 6-game winning streak over their arch rivals.

"There's not a stigma or anything," said Tar Heel guard Darrell Elston, who tossed in 23 points Tuesday night. "I think we'll play well over at Raleigh; we usually do. I really believe we can beat them."

Chapter 31

Raising hell in the dark

Shortly after the Wolfpack defeated Carolina in Chapel Hill, around 11:10 that Tuesday night, the State campus went dark. It wasn't a way to control the on-campus celebration of the win over the Tar Heels. There was a "malfunction in a primary switch gear system", according to campus authorities, that caused the lights to go out. A backup system was put into place to replace the new switch, which had been operating for only three weeks.

But that didn't stop the students from partying. It just changed the way they celebrated, as reported in "Students raise hell during blackout," by staff writer Howard Barnett:

> The atmosphere was one of general mayhem.
>
> The streets, halls, and sidewalks were filled with thousands of State students busily engaged in raising all kinds and degrees of hell. They were celebrating State's victory over Carolina, and the spirit was one of pure glee. Horns blew, fireworks went off, and trees anywhere in the general vicinity of students took on the look of a winter wonderland as layer upon layer of toilet paper decorated their branches, a practice now traditional.
>
> Then, suddenly, in the midst of the celebration, the entire campus went black. At first the reaction was one of general

annoyance. It was presumed that residence life, or the head residence counselor, or that stupid floor jock had thought it could preserve order by dousing the lights.

As time wore on, though, people discovered that the power outage wasn't restricted only to their dorm, that residence life and security were baffled, and nobody knew what was wrong. Then the mood turned to malevolence. What things might one do under cover of darkness?

The answer came soon. The Lee-Sullivan-Bragaw area, a battleground at its best, became unfit for human habitation. Beer cans, bottles, and various other articles sailed off the topmost floors into the night. Powerful flashlights searched the surrounding area, picking out those fools who chose to go into, out of, or around the buildings. The area on the south end of Bragaw was caught in a crossfire of firecrackers, bottle rockets, M-80s, and sparklers. On at least two occasions, a toilet paper-laden tree caught fire from the sparks. A water fountain in the lobby was turned over and flooded the area with about three inches of water.

A number of people were trapped in elevators in Lee and Sullivan. When the power went back on, they found others waiting for them when they got off—with trash cans full of water.

No serious injuries were reported in spite of all this, and when the lights finally came on, most of the student body was in one piece or so. The blackout, which was originally attributed to everything from a trash can or wire thrown into the substation beside Bragaw to a Carolina sabotage plot, turned out to be the result of equipment failure.

There were reports of fires in a couple of windows because of the candles, but no serious damage was incurred.

Students woke up the next morning with hangovers, fatigue, and in general, one hell of a mess to clean up.

And, in an editorial, "Werewolves," the *Technician's* opinion writers chimed in on the student conduct during the blackout:

...to those who perpetrated these acts, these might have seemed mere pranks, but objects falling several stories through the air can gain quite a bit of momentum before they hit the ground—or the person. Serious injuries might have occurred—but fortunately did not—due to these shenanigans. These people should have considered the consequences in full before taking part in such juvenile behavior.

College students should by now have enough maturity to judge for themselves what is and what is not a threat to the safety of others. It is hard to believe that so many people on campus have so little respect for others.

The campus was probably fortunate that the blackout did not occur while the State-Carolina game was being transmitted. It's scary to think what might have happened then. There probably wouldn't be a campus left if these people had been mad instead of happy.

The success of the basketball team was front and center on campus, and next up for the Wolfpack was a trip to Purdue. The Boilermakers were coming off a 1-point win over Michigan, which put Purdue at the top of the Big Ten Conference standings.

Coach Norm Sloan was guarded in his pre-game assessment of the challenge ahead. "We will have our hands full," he said. "They are gathering momentum with each game and are getting better and better. They have a very talented basketball team. (John) Garrett is a big forward and is their fire power. (Frank) Kendrick is an experienced front line performer. And their backcourt (Bruce Parkinson and Jerry Nichols) has more power than anyone we will play."

Whether it was good play by Purdue or over confidence by State, the Wolfpack struggled against the Boilermakers, trailing by 15 points with about 17 minutes to go in the game.

Chapter 32

Wolfpack overcomes Boilermakers

Reprinted from the Technician, January 28, 1974

By Jim Pomeranz

Sports Editor

WEST LAFAYETTE, IN—They came here to win, and they did—86–81.

State's Wolfpack basketball team flew in here Friday around midafternoon for a Saturday evening televised contest with the Purdue Boilermakers. Reports on Purdue scouted them to be tough, and the Boilermakers were definitely that.

This Midwestern town, with a population of 45,000 (which includes 25,000 Boilermakers), is not in the exact center of basketball country (Indiana), but after a close ball game with the Big Ten Conference leaders, the Pack realized the quality played there.

"Nobody has played a half against us all year as well as they did," commented Norm Sloan after the comeback victory. "The type of ball they played was really good."

Sloan was speaking, of course, about the first half of play when Purdue players hit 19 of 43 shots from the floor, 11 of 19 tries from the charity stripe, and held a commanding 49–39 halftime lead. It was the first time this season the Wolfpack has been trailing at the midway buzzer.

Purdue jumped off to a quick 7–0 lead in the early goings and led all the way until the 3:19 mark of the second half. That was when a layup by State guard Morris Rivers and a following free throw brought the Pack even with the Boilermakers, 81–81. Before that mark, State could manage to pull only within one; that happened only once, and that was only after the first 4 minutes of the game had been played.

After tying Purdue, the Pack "teased" the Boilermakers the rest of the way to gain the win.

Throughout the game, State's players looked a little sluggish, and there were times when lack of movement was evident.

"Both of us had our minds on conference play, not taking anything away from Purdue," offered Sloan after the contest. "We were coming off Carolina and thinking about Maryland (Wednesday night)." Purdue had just won a big conference game over rival Michigan.

"Purdue played well and shot well," he added. "They definitely outplayed us in the first half."

To counter the slow moving Pack, Sloan used the services of always spunky forward Greg Hawkins.

"I looked down the bench and saw him (Hawkins)," said the State head mentor. "He looked like he wanted to play, so I put him in. It's what we needed. The only reason I took him out was that he looked tired, but I put him right back in."

Hawkins scored 3 points and pulled down 3 important rebounds in the 19 minutes he played.

High man for the victorious Pack was once again All-American Dave Thompson with 26 points. Thompson went scoreless for the first 16 minutes of the contest, but once he got started, Purdue could not stop him.

"He made the difference in the second half," commented Purdue head coach Fred Schaus about the Shelby native. "Anytime you go

111

close to the wire and you have the superstar, you win. He is one fine basketball player."

Guard Monte Towe followed Thompson in the scoring column for State with 18 points. The Converse, IN, native had praise for the Boilermakers.

"They played as good a game as they have played all year," said the 5'7" court general. "I knew they were good, but I didn't expect them to play that well.

"It was one of the worst starts we've had," Towe added. "We never did play well all night. We just came up with the big play at the right time. It's good to know you can play like that and still win though."

One of the most interesting results of the game was the domination of the board by State's Tom Burleson. The 7'4" center played for only 16 minutes against Purdue but managed to pull down 17 rebounds. One rebound came with only 1 minute left in the game and the Pack ahead 83–81. After that rebound, the Pack's Rivers drew a foul and put State out in front by 3.

On the following Purdue possession, the towering Burleson blocked a shot to keep the Boilermakers from pulling up to the Pack. Burleson was third in scoring for the Pack with 13 points.

The State center's counterpart, John Garrett, was the story for the Boilermakers. The 6'11" junior tossed in 24 points for Purdue, 18 of which came in the first period.

Sloan was pleased with the end play of Burleson against Garrett, but during the first half, according to Sloan, "Garrett ate him alive."

Forward Frank Kendrick followed Garrett in Purdue scoring with 19 points.

Chapter 33

Covering SPORTS: A beautiful technical foul

Reprinted from the Technician, January 30, 1974

By Jim Pomeranz

Sports Editor

WEST LAFAYETTE, Ind.—Even though it took 38 minutes for State to edge ahead of Purdue here Saturday afternoon, it seemed like the Pack might be handed its second loss of the season for most of the game.

What goes through a Wolfpack supporter's mind when he sees his team down by 15 points with only 17 minutes to play? The last time State was down by that many was that disastrous day back in December over in nearby St. Louis.

How does a reporter write about his team when it loses? With the exception of the UCLA game, State has not lost a game over the past two seasons; and winning has become such a tradition, I have forgotten how to create such a story on the Wolfpack basketball team.

State did win the ball game (86–81), and, of course, that was exciting to watch. The Pack looked great coming from behind. I knew we were headed for victory when State assistant athletic director Frank Weedon leaned over and pronounced, "We're gonna win!" That came when the Pack trailed by only 6 and there was a little over 6 minutes remaining. What the heck, a point a minute is not so bad.

*   *   *   *

Mackey Arena is one whale of a place to play basketball. The circular monstrosity seats 14,123 screaming fans according to the fire marshal, but according to sources nearer the scene, the complex seats a little under 16,000.

The seats do not have backs for the big contributors to sit back in, and the students do not need them with all the standing, and sitting, and yelling they do.

*   *   *   *

Either the playing surface itself is above the floor of the arena, or the floor is below the playing surface, but anyway, the two are not on the same level. It makes for an interesting situation at times.

For instance, the most beautiful technical foul was called on Purdue coach Fred Schaus (if a technical foul can be said to have any beauty to it), and it was because of the floor.

At State, when a coach stands up to converse with the official, he sort of blends in with the team and the crowd. But at Purdue, the coach came right up onto the floor, and when the official turned and saw him talking about the ref's heritage or something—ZAP! Technical foul it was.

*   *   *   *

Purdue University is located in the city of West Lafayette, Indiana. As one official describes the population in the area, "Lafayette itself has 60,000 people, West Lafayette 20,000, and Purdue 25,000."

The two cities are divided by the Wabash River. Yes, there is actually a river named after the "Wabash Cannonball."

When it was discovered that there was a Wabash River, Charlie Harvell of WGHP-TV in High Point, and one of the announcers for last Saturday's game, suggested that he could sing the "Wabash Cannonball" for the halftime entertainment on the broadcast. Most observers felt they were fortunate to be watching the game live.

*   *   *   *

As the State team was entering the arena before the game, a small group of Indiana natives gathered and began to wish Monte Towe well in the game. Towe is from Converse, Indiana.

One fan asked the small guard what he thought about returning home to play. "I don't like it," Towe laughingly answered.

Maybe he knew something about the game that others did not.

Chapter 34

The right perspective

Four days later, the Wolfpack had a rematch with Maryland, this time at College Park and the second between State and the Terps in 17 days. The Wolfpack was now in the second spot in the national basketball polls and was looking for a fifth straight win over Maryland. Coach Norm Sloan knew of the game's importance.

"Maryland is a very important basketball game for both of us," Sloan was quoted in a game-day story. "If we could win at Maryland, it would put us in a wonderful position as far as the regular season race is concerned. As far as Maryland is concerned, they must look at it as a must game because they have already lost two conference games. This would be third loss for them, and it would be their second loss to us. We know Lefty (Driesell) will have his basketball team ready, and their fans have been looking forward to this game. We have always had difficulty with (Tom) McMillen, and we know that John Lucas will give us problems again. Every time we have played against Maryland, he (McMillen) has scored in the 20s and such is the case with John Lucas."

The game was originally scheduled to start at 9:00 p.m. but was moved to a 7:00 p.m. start to avoid conflict with President Nixon's annual State of the Union address to congress. This prompted at least one State student to comment, "We have to get our perspective right

116

around here. Since when do more people want to hear the president instead of the State-Maryland game?"

On the State campus, probably no one wanted to hear the president, especially considering the results of the game. The students were celebrating a spectacular David Thompson performance.

Chapter 35

David Thompson shoots down Terps

Reprinted from the Technician, February 1, 1974

By Jim Pomeranz

Sports Editor

COLLEGE PARK, MD—*The David Thompson Basketball Show* played in College Park Wednesday night and, after a slow start, put on one of the most "dazzlin'" performances ever to be witnessed.

The leading role of the number 2 nationally ranked Wolfpack review was, of course, that man about the court who always seems to come through in the clutch, David Thompson.

He started out slow in the first half of the production hitting only 4 of 11 shots from the floor for 8 points and pulling down 2 rebounds.

But after intermission, in which many critics were weary of his production, Thompson performed with a flair that would gain an Emmy for his leading role in a television show, a Tony for fantastic stage-play acting, and an Oscar for a performance that one would only see in the movies.

The self-made hero really sparkled in the second act that night.

Thompson attempted 15 shots against many helpless adversaries in that final 20 minutes of action and was true on 12 of the 2-point tosses. The Shelby native also scored 7 1-point tosses while attempting

10. His final total of 39 points was his second high of his Wolfpack career.

"David was tremendous," raved State head coach Norm Sloan after the Wolfpack had handed Maryland its third conference loss of the season and the second by State, 86–80.

"They put fresh people on him every chance they could," he continued, "but David can be successful against anyone." The Terrapins challenged Thompson with Tom Roy, Tom McMillen, Owen Brown, and Len Elmore. As it turned out, each of those Maryland players finished up the game with 4 fouls.

Back on Super Sunday, Roy was one of the victims that had the opportunity to guard the fantastic State junior. He scored in that game, too, putting in 41 points. Roy was awed by the most recent performance of Thompson.

"During the first half, he was hurting us at critical times with just a basket here or there," explained the 6'9" junior, "but not like he did in the second half. He came out and sort of unconsciously made them.

"He was cold at first, but then Thompson just started hitting again," Roy said in amazement. "There is no sense in it at all. He was just throwing them up, and they were going in."

Thompson began his surge of second half points with jumpers from "way out in downtown Washington somewhere," but then as the State team moved into its tease offensive pattern, layups became the scoring route.

"In the first half, it was hard and physical," said the State All-American. "I was looser in the second half. I could get off my jumper, and then I had my man one-on-one near the end and could drive on him."

The Maryland encounter was probably the roughest game played by State in quite a while, and Thompson knew it as he described it being "rough, especially on the boards."

And Thompson was definitely on the boards. The high leaping guard-forward-center all rolled into one, at one time while trying for a layup, jumped so high that when the Terrapin's Len Elmore attempted to block the shot, Thompson's side just above the rib cage was pinned against the backboard.

But as always, a movie, a play, or a television show not only needs a star but also a supporting cast can be helpful. Behind the talented Thompson were guards Morris Rivers and Monte Towe each scoring 16 points. Towe and Rivers took toward the basket when Thompson was tied up, which was rarely. Tom Burleson, who had been sick for most of the day Wednesday before the game, tossed in 11 points for the Wolfpack while pulling down 13 rebounds.

And, of course, there are the villains to any story. Sloan had praise for the Terrapins performance in the television highlight of the evening.

"Maryland played extremely well," he said. "They just moved the ball around until they found the open man."

The open man was usually 6'11" Tom McMillen, who tossed in 28 points for the losers and pulled down 14 rebounds. If it was not the senior forward-center, then it was Durham's John Lucas, who scored 21 points for Maryland.

The David Thompson Basketball Show has been making believers out of many basketball fans for the last two seasons, and for Maryland fans, that happened Wednesday night. The voice of Roy, though, has still not been affected as he stated, "I've seen one better—(UCLA's Bill) Walton."

Chapter 36

After the riot?

Usually when athletics is blamed for something, it has negative connotations. In early February, it was reported that applications for enrollment at State for the fall of 1974 were showing a big increase over previous years, and Dr. Thomas Stafford, director of Student Affairs Research, gave some of the credit for increased interest to athletics.

"One factor undoubtedly is the success of our athletics program and the attention and the publicity they've generated for the school. I think we've probably had more success than any other school in the state and gotten more publicity through that," he told *Technician* staff writer Sheryl Lieb.

The Wolfpack's on the field success was also having an impact on football recruiting. It was signing time, and football coach Lou Holtz had convinced quarterback-tailback Johnny Evans of High Point to sign with State. "He is a fine all-around athlete, and he has great character," Said Holtz. Evans had narrowed his choices to State and Carolina. The Tar Heels dangled the prestigious Morehead Scholarship in front of him, but Evans, voted the Carolinas' outstanding high school athlete, chose the Wolfpack primarily because of Holtz's veer offense.

While the success was positive in one way, actions around the basketball coach rubbed some people—writers in particular—another way. On February 1 the *Technician* reprinted an article by Joe Creason, a sports columnist for the Louisville *Courier-Journal,* who took on the behavior of the home crowd at the early January game when Maryland visited State's Reynolds Coliseum. Creason wrote:

> Maybe I'm being like a malfunctioning clock and just getting alarmed over nothing, but it seems to me that the behavior of crowds at college basketball games this season has reached an all-time low.
>
> All of which gives a team playing at home an unfair advantage that is enjoyed in no other sport.
>
> It used to be that in nearly every conference there was one gym that visiting teams referred to as "the snake pit" because of the venomous attitude of the home spectators. Today, nearly every court is a snake pit for visitors, and even a nationally-ranked team that wins half its away games against relative patsies regards its season a great success.
>
> The team that loses on the road, of course, expects full retribution when the tormentors play in its own snake pit.
>
> The Maryland at North Carolina State game … provided a perfect "showcase" for the ridiculously hostile attitude of many home-team fans. As each Maryland player was introduced, instead of a semi-polite patter of applause or even silence, the crowd erupted in loud boos. NC State cheerleaders led the home folks in raucous "Go to hell, Maryland. Go to hell" yells. When Maryland players stepped to the free throw line, the crowd whistled shrilly, and fans behind the goal arose and waved arms, programs or pompoms to distract the shooter.

Unfortunately, that game wasn't an isolated exception of fan behavior; the fact it was on national TV simply made it a glaring example of how any trace of crowd sportsmanship has been lost.

What to do about this? Crowd behavior, I'm told, is the responsibility of the home coach. In view of this, I'd like to see some brave soul go to the microphone at the first shout of "go to hell" and plainly tell the crowd that if it doesn't shape up, he'll take his team off the floor and forfeit the game.

Such shock treatment might work—after the riot.

Leading into the reprint, the *Technician* included its own appeal to State students for better behavior: "With a televised home game with Virginia tomorrow, State fans can show the other side of sportsmanship, the "good" side that outside viewers such as Mr. Creason claim we don't have. Bad sportsmanship did not start in Reynolds Coliseum but good sportsmanship can."

Did the students take to heart the comments by Mr. Creason? Sort of. State was trying to run its overall mark to 15–1 and ACC record to 8–0 against the Cavaliers in Reynolds Coliseum, and it needed the rowdy fans in a supporting role as well as good play from players. And, two days later, the Wolfpack found a hostile crowd at Duke taking aim at the misfortunes of Morris Rivers but knew that winning would quiet the crowd.

Chapter 37

Covering SPORTS: Hoop 'n hollera

Reprinted from the Technician, February 4, 1974

By Jim Pomeranz

Sports Editor

The article entitled "Reynolds becomes 'snake pit'" in last Friday's *Technician* made me think back to the State-Maryland game in College Park last Wednesday and cite just how the Terrapin crowd treated the visiting Wolfpack.

As I best recall, the fans there were just as "terrible" as those in Reynolds. Those "lunatic" Maryland fans screamed and waved their hands as well as any Atlantic Coast Conference fan throughout the seven schools could when State players were shooting free throws.

At the slightest close call by an official against the Maryland team, the fans turned into wild animals. They threw ice and cups at the refs and onto the floor and yelled obscenities at those men in black-and-white striped shirts.

When the announcer made a plea to the fans to stop their childish actions, there were no results. As a matter of fact, when the plea was made for no more tossing of cups and ice, just the opposite occurred.

And to add flame to the fire, Maryland coach Lefty Driesell helped by motioning to the crowd for loud yelling and throwing. After a foul had been called on a Terrapin, Driesell stood up and waved his hands high above his head (like a good Baptist preacher might do on Sunday morning), and so did the fans. Then they began to ask the refs about the call—in various ways, of course.

It seems like all fans throughout the ACC act the same at basketball games.

But I also observed the crowd at the State-Virginia game Saturday, and I must say that the students were much better. The hand waving was completely gone, except for maybe one or two people, and the yelling at the ref was a little less.

But one group of people I noticed most was that group that sits in the upper section and pays all that money into athletic scholarships. We all know them as the Wolfpack Club.

There were two men in section five who gave the refs pure hell the whole game and rarely gave praise for the basketball players' feats out on the court.

Their yelling, which goes practically unnoticed since it is so far from the court, went something like this:

"Come on, ref, he's walking all over the place."

"Stick to high school ref."

Those statements came after a State player clearly fouled a Virginia player and the Cavalier was on the line shooting a free throw. The conversation continued:

"You're allowed five (players) Gibson."

"Yeah, take your time. Ha! Ha!"

This poking fun at the Virginia coach occurred after one of his players had fouled out, and Bill Gibson was just taking the allotted time replacing him.

And then there was the cry of "you're real consistent ref. We know you can't see." Then the two men looked at each other as if they had accomplished something.

These two men never once stood up to praise the Pack. I wonder if they stood up for the national anthem. Even when the starting five State players were replaced, very little reaction came from the two "supporters." One of them gave a chuckle at the second five State players now on the court, and the other looked as if he really did not care.

We definitely need cheering from the crowd at basketball games, but there is no real reason to yell at the refs the way many people do. However, we do not need the type of fans that I observed in the upper deck last Saturday. That kind of ref reaction and that type of player non-reaction is uncalled for.

The ACC is the best basketball conference in the nation, and the home-team fans are what make it what it is.

As one bystander put it, "the ACC would not be the same without the hoop 'n hollera that is now present at each of the schools in the conference."

Chapter 38

Wolfpack eight lead win

Reprinted from the Technician, February 4, 1974

By Bill Moss

Staff Writer

Behind every great basketball team there stands a bench stocked with quality players who can be counted on to come into a game and contribute to the team effort. Virginia learned that State is no exception to the rule as the Cavaliers fell to the Wolfpack, 105–93, in a run and gun contest Saturday afternoon.

Three Wolfpack players who did not start the game—Mark Moeller, Steve Nuce, and Phil Spence—came off the bench and combined for 24 points, nearly a fourth of the team's scoring. Moreover, their combined percentage from the floor was an impressive 61%.

Spence, a 6'8" junior college transfer, has started a few games this season for State. He admits there's a difference in coming off the bench or starting.

"It's just psychologically different," said Spence. "Starting makes you feel like you're one of the main guys."

But when Spence goes in the game as a reserve, the forward-center tries to perform as if he were there all the time.

"I just go in there to keep it going," he explained about the action on the court. "I come in to keep doing what Tim (Stoddard) was doing."

Mark Moeller looks at the situation as a team effort.

"My goal is to help the team," said the 6'3" junior guard. "It's always nice to start, but Morris (Rivers) is doing a great job, and he deserves to be starting."

The Canfield, Ohio, native came off the bench against Virginia and hit 3 out of 3 shots from the floor. For him, coming off the bench means getting involved in the game. "If you've been sitting on the bench, you might be a little tight. I just get in there, get involved, and adapt to the situation," commented Moeller.

For his supporting role in the Virginia game, Steve Nuce scored 10 points and pulled down 9 rebounds. "Sometimes you get a little bit more excited if you're starting," he said. "It's kind of an honor to be put ahead of the other guys."

Nuce allows that being taken out of the game affects him somewhat. "It has got to be a little bit frustrating," explained the 6'8" senior. "But you just got to have respect for coach Sloan and know that you're gonna be back in there."

Nuce, a deadly shooter, said he likes taking the outside shot. "I have a lot of confidence in my shooting, and I feel natural taking it. If somebody leaves me open, I'm gonna take the shot," he added.

Tim Stoddard, Nuce, and Spence have all started at the forward position at one time or another this season. Stoddard drew the starting assignment against Virginia and responded by turning in his best performance of the season. He canned 16 points—many of those on shots from deep in the corner—and had 8 rebounds.

According to the husky junior, a good game is the result of working hard on the basketball floor. "At the beginning of the year, I was playing really bad," Stoddard said after his Saturday performance.

"The last 3 or 4 games I really played good. I was working hard. The coach told me just to work hard and things will start happening," he continued. "That's what happened today."

The Wolfpack travels to Durham tonight to face another ACC foe. Duke is always tough at home, and Norman Sloan is one man that will not take the game lightly. "I'm really worried about the Duke game," he said. "They're waiting to jump all over someone."

Coach Neil McGeachy's Blue Devils are led by Bob Fleisher, Chris Redding, and Kevin Billerman. After losing to Maryland 104–83 at College Park Saturday, Duke would like to have a big win at home.

But to defeat State, the Duke team must contend with the Pack's talented "starting eight."

Chapter 39

Letters to the editor

Included in the highlights of a student newspaper are the letters to the editor from students who are passionate for what they believe, giving extra credit when such should be awarded and taking aim at frustrations when, well, something moves them to write, let's say, passionately.

For instance, in the giving credit when due category, there was a letter written by David French, a communications sophomore. Titled, "Thanks, Tim," it was timed accordingly to follow the story about the Wolfpack's win over Virginia, written by Bill Moss. Here's the letter, published in the February 11 edition, a week after the fact:

> Last Saturday's basketball game against Virginia exemplifies the fine, all-around talented basketball team that is State. As Bill Moss so aptly stated it "...a bench stocked with quality players who can be counted on ...to contribute to the team effort."
>
> That was evident in the outstanding performances of some members of the squad who don't see action on the court so frequently as others. Sloan's decision to start Tim Stoddard was sheer genius—and Tim didn't disappoint him of the State fans. It was truly a pleasure to watch him play, as it is watching any

talented basketball player—and we are blessed with many fine players like Stoddard!

My point is this—surely we have excellent players in Thompson, Burleson, and Towe—and we should be and are proud of what they've done for State's basketball program. Our other regular starters are equally as talented and versatile as those mentioned above, to say the least. But when a player like Tim Stoddard performs against Virginia as he did, then that's really something to be proud of. Let's remember that those guys who aren't always in the limelight are darn good basketball players in their own right, and deserve some of the credit for making the team as great as it is. Now I can refute the argument of some of my friends who aren't State fans (which is tragic) hold to be true: that our team is carried by two or three players. Thanks, Tim, and you other guys who make it easier for them to see that they've been dead wrong.

Stoddard, as Moss pointed out, had 16 points and 8 rebounds against Virginia. French's letter was a celebration of good talent that gained few headlines. On the other hand, in the being passionate about frustrations, several days later, John Nantz, a senior majoring in civil engineering, was ecstatic that the Wolfpack was dominating our cousins from Chapel Hill, and he showed his disdain for the Tar Heel and for anyone who thought State's Reynolds Coliseum fans shouldn't be rude to Carolina, soon to visit the Wolfpack. His letter titled "Hell with 'em" was printed in the *Technician's* February 20 edition. It followed the appearance of light blue graffiti plastered on specific walls and buildings.

I attended State from 1965 to 1967, served three years in the Army from 1967 to 1970, and then came back to State in 1970. I will graduate in May of this year. Although during three of my years at State the athletics program was average I was one of the Pack's most loyal supporters. During my last two years at State the athletic program has been the best in the nation in my opinion.

From 1965 until 1972 I waited patiently for the Pack to gain the national prominence it now has. It seemed during this time Carolina dominated the scene. I caught a lot of BS and grief from many Carolina fans and their offspring. Now that the shoe is on the other foot I won't take it anymore.

The minority who feel that Pack backers don't act correctly at basketball games must not have seen the baby blue paint scrawled on the Coliseum, the gym, the natatorium, the Technician boxes, the Coliseum tunnel, the Supply Store, and everywhere else. Trivia such as this does nothing to help my relations with Carolina. Fact is, it causes me to despise the place even more than I do now. Rest assured the Heels will know I'm there and how I feel next time they're in Reynolds Coliseum at the same time I am, which should be soon.

Then there are those who are "disappointed" by the reception given friends from Chapel Hill by State students. Actually, we'd rather they stay in Chapel Hill where they want to be. However, should they return to Raleigh, you and your friend should walk down to the Coliseum and take a good look at the paint spattered on the campus by those who would rather be in Chapel Hill. I'm sure you and your friend will understand why the majority of State students hold Carolina students in such low esteem. If you don't understand, perhaps you'd like to remove the paint anyway.

I've read letters from Carolina students bitching about the way State students used to bitch. Who's bitching, man?

There there's the little girl who wants to know why almost all State basketball games are televised now and hardly any Carolina games. After all, weren't more Carolina games televised in the past than State games?

I love it! I love to hear Woody Durham say, "Well, Dean, there were a few questionable calls in that loss to the Pack!" I love to read where Smith Barrier writes, "Pack Does The Impossible For Sixth Time In A Row!" I just love it to death!

Go to hell, Carolina, go to Hell! The Pack is the best, to hell with the rest!

The Tar Heels would be visiting Reynolds Coliseum just six days after that letter was printed. Between Stoddard's play against Virginia February 2 and the February 26 meeting with the Tar Heels, The Wolfpack continued to win while UCLA, the nation's top team, lost twice and State found itself elevated to No. 1 in the polls.

Chapter 40

Pack 'exorcises' Devils

Reprinted from the Technician, February 6, 1974

By Ken Lloyd

Associate Sports Editor

DURHAM—When State's basketball team was introduced Monday night in Duke's Cameron Indoor Stadium, the Wolfpack starting five were showered with aspirin by the raucous and rude Blue Devil fans.

But as it turned out, the Duke faithful should have saved the aspirin for the outmanned Blue Devil players as the streaking Wolfpack raced to a convincing 92–78 victory.

State started off rather sluggishly, as has been the custom in the past few games. For the first 11 minutes, the Blue Devils stayed close as they moved the ball well on offense and took the percentage shot.

But State's strength and balance soon became evident as the Pack pulled away in the latter part of the first half and coasted home for the win, the Wolfpack's 16th of the season.

"We had some good moments out there, although we were a little sloppy at times," said coach Norm Sloan. "When you get ahead like we did (22 points at one time), you sometimes tend to get complacent, and that may have happened to us."

In the contest, tall Tommy Burleson was awesome, smooth Morris Rivers went to the basket like a magnet, diminutive Monte Towe wowed the crowd with his ball handling and shooting, and David Thompson was, well, just David Thompson.

Burleson had what Sloan called "one of his best" games ever. He dominated play at both ends of the court like he is capable of doing in just about every outing.

Hitting on 9 of 15 shots from the floor, Burleson scored 18 points, and also pulled down 15 rebounds and rejected 6 of the Blue Devils' shots. All this transpired despite the fact he fouled out of the contest with over 8 minutes remaining in the game.

"I thought Tommy was tremendous," praised Sloan. "He remembered the first time he came over here as a freshman. He played one of his worst basketball games since he has been at State. Tonight, he played maybe his best."

"That game was in the back of my mind," Burleson admitted. "I fouled out, and I think their center (Dave Elmer) got about 40 points. I wanted to leave here (Cameron Stadium) with a clear conscience, just like I left at (Carolina's) Carmichael Auditorium."

Thompson went about his business Monday night in an uncustomary unspectacular manner. His 24 points and 13 rebounds were relatively unnoticed compared to Burleson's accomplishments.

Rivers, who seems to move effortlessly on both offense and defense, had his best game of the season scoring-wise. He poured in 18 points, with many coming in slick moves around the basket.

"Morris keeps improving with every game," lauded teammate Towe, who finished up with 12 points. "He hasn't been intimidated yet. He looks like a seasoned veteran out here."

Now the Wolfpack gets a two week break from Atlantic Coast Conference wars. State travels to Charlotte to battle Georgia Tech and

Furman, and then entertains Davidson next weekend before battling Wake Forest at home on February 16.

"We can relax a little now since this is the last pressure game for us for a while," said Sloan. "Lately, it seemed like every game was a big one."

With the win over Duke, the Pack has now beaten every conference team at least once, with 4 of the wins coming on the road.

"I said before the season, we had 12 big games," maintained Sloan. "Now we have 5 left.

"I feel good about our basketball team," the coach continued. "We're getting better every time we go out there."

Chapter 41

Fitting the bill of student interest

In a letter to the *(Technician)* editor (published February 6), junior Mike Fahey crystallized the importance of sports on the campus. He was reacting to the cancelation of All Campus, a major annual two-day concert that was halted due to lack of funds. He wrote, "All Campus the last two years was something that every student on campus could enjoy. Furthermore, these little events (schedule in its place) seem to be aimed for specialized groups, which tend to fragment the campus down into little groups. As things stand, the only thing which attracts a majority of students is sports."

Specifically, at this time of year, the basketball team fit the bill.

The basketball team was 16–1 and headed to Charlotte for the annual North-South Doubleheader, a two-day event that initially include State and North Carolina playing games against Clemson and South Carolina. Over time, the opponents changed, and this year the Wolfpack would play Georgia Tech and Furman, two nonconference teams, on back-to-back nights.

"These games are important," said coach Norm Sloan, "and we're going to Charlotte to win. But the strain of playing ACC teams has been tremendous, and we need a mental rest. I said before the season that our number one priority was to win our league games and number two, the ACC championship. I know Georgia Tech and Furman will come after us awfully hard, but I'm confident our squad will be ready. Playing outside opposition simply does not carry the same pressure that is there when you play a conference game. The break in the schedule should be good for us."

So were the results.

Chapter 42

Pack smashes Ga Tech, Furman in North-South

Reprinted from the Technician, February 11, 1974

By Bill Moss

Staff Writer

The teams from the North just had too much. The teams from the South had too little. And the sixteenth annual North-South Doubleheader ended with 4 more routs in the record book.

The official program lauded the doubleheader saying that "there's a better than 50% chance that…you'll see one or more games go to the wire before determining the winner." But, oh, how wrong it was.

State defeated Georgia Tech, 98–54, Friday night and downed Furman, 111–91, Saturday night. Carolina also had no trouble with the South as they outscored the Purple Paladins, 95–69, Friday evening and easily finished off the Yellow Jackets, 112–70, Saturday in the night cap.

About the only suspenseful moments came near the end of the Wolfpack's game with Furman when fans wondered if State would reach the century mark on the scoreboard. The Wolfpack had more trouble escaping autograph seekers than they did scoring on the southern teams.

The trio of David Thompson, Tommy Burleson, and Monte Towe once again did most of the damage for the Pack. Thompson wowed the capacity crowd with moves that would have shamed Allied Van Lines. Burleson rebounded, blocked shots, and scored 38 points in the 2 games. And Towe amazed fans with those bombs from somewhere in downtown Charlotte.

Thompson collected 46 points for the weekend while pulling down 13 rebounds, and Towe tossed in 38 points against Furman and Georgia Tech. Burleson hauled down 22 rebounds during the 2-day stand.

State's little general also fired court-length passes for easy layups and came up with just about every loose ball like a vacuum cleaner picks up dirt. Towe, at times, completely marveled the crowd.

At one point, with State well out in front of Furman, Towe sped to the basket for an easy layup, and, instead of taking the shot, he lobbed the ball backwards to the onrushing Thompson, who put it in for 2 more points.

The combined 4 wins for the Wolfpack and the Tar Heels gives those 2 teams a combined record of 48–16 in the North-South Doubleheader. Not since 1971 has a team outside of North Carolina won a game in this annual event, and there seems to be no end in sight for the southern teams' losing ways.

It's those lopsided records that make people wonder why this event continues each year.

Furman head coach Joe Williams sees the Charlotte event as a learning process for his team. "The reason we play in these games is to see if we can improve," he said after Saturday's game with State. "We judge our program by how well we do in them. We try to get used to playing outstanding teams.

"This is like a dry run for our tournament play," he continued. "If we can play well against these teams, our players will realize how well they can play against conference teams."

140

Tar Heel coach Dean Smith does not mind bringing his team to the doubleheader either. "It's a great trip to Charlotte," he said, "and it's good for the Carolina fans in Charlotte who can't see us play in Carmichael Auditorium. I saw some good basketball out there tonight, and I'm sure the fans did too."

For the ACC players, the North-South Doubleheader provides a welcomed break from the tough ACC competition.

"It's a good tournament because we had a good break from our conference games," commented Carolina sophomore Mitch Kupchak. "It's really like a break in the season. And it's good for the fans, too. They get to see a doubleheader, and they get to see two ACC teams play two nonconference teams. I'm sure they enjoy it."

Towe likes the 2-day affair because it allows the team to relax a little. "It's not as much pressure as it used to be when South Carolina and Clemson were here," said the State junior. "We just go out and relax and have fun."

The fans that packed the Charlotte Coliseum did not see 4 good basketball games. They did not even get to see 1, but they did have the opportunity to see 2 of the nation's best teams in State and Carolina.

And for the Wolfpack fans in particular they once again got to see Thompson's "ballerina-like" moves, Burleson's play in the pivot, and Towe's 30-foot jumpers that go "zing." Maybe the North-South Doubleheader is worth it after all.

Chapter 43

Morris Rivers *nol prossed*

On Monday, February 11, Morris Rivers, charged in early January with shoplifting a tin of aspirin from a convenience store, had his day in court. The *Technician* did not have a reporter present at the hearing, which had been moved ahead of its originally scheduled date.

Coach Norm Sloan criticized the newspaper for not covering the hearing while making the arrest the lead story. Rivers was not only given his day in court but also in an above-the-banner article accompanied by a sizeable photo in the Wednesday, February 13 edition.

Back on the sports page, the back page of the *Technician,* the Wolfpack basketball team was getting ready for another nonconference game. This time is was a Wednesday night game at home against Davidson coached by Terry Holland, whose Wildcats that season had defeated Wake Forest and Virginia and lost to Duke. State, with 26 points from Joe Cafferky who was recovering from pneumonia, defeated Davidson the year before, 103–90, in Charlotte.

An interesting note came out of the State Sports Information Department that week. Since donning a Wolfpack varsity uniform in the fall of 1972, David Thompson had been the team's scoring leader.

The game against Davidson wasn't close, and it was followed by a Saturday home game against Wake Forest. Also that weekend, which State entered as the nation's second-ranked team, No. 1 UCLA lost twice, elevating the Wolfpack to the top.

Chapter 44

District Attorney drops Rivers case

Reprinted from the Technician, February 13, 1974

By Jim Pomeranz

Sports Editor

The shoplifting charge against State basketball player Morris Rivers was *nol prossed* Monday morning in district court here. According to Burley B. Mitchell, Jr., district attorney for the tenth district, the charges were dropped because of lack of evidence.

Rivers had been charged with shoplifting a 37-cent box of Anacin from the Mission Valley Convenient Food Mart on Monday, January 14. The charge was filed by a private security guard.

"I *nol prossed* it on the grounds that we (the state) could not convict on the charge and certainly not before a jury. It would be incredible that a man would steal 37 cents worth of aspirin when he could go to the trainer and get $37 worth if he wanted it," Mitchell said.

Mitchell stated that he had talked to "all witnesses," and that he had then decided there was insufficient evidence.

"His (Rivers') girl in the car said he had walked out to the car and asked for some change to pay for the aspirin," continued the district attorney. "With that and other statements, we could not show or prove any intent to steal."

Mitchell also stated that the warrant under which Rivers had been charged was defective and would have to have been changed in court.

Nol prossed simply means that the prosecutor decided not to pursue the case any further than it had been pursued already.

Mitchell explained that his opinion was that the state could not find Rivers guilty and therefore the case was dismissed.

Chapter 45

Sorrentino: Pack, Notre Dame even

From the Technician, February 15, 1974

By Ray Deltz

Staff Writer

Shooting 67% in the first half, the Wolfpack quickly indicated that they would add Davidson as their third victim of their "fun games," which began last week against Georgia Tech and Furman. By outhustling, outshooting, and generally outplaying the Wildcats, the Wolfpack gave notice that they are fully prepared for their remaining ACC warfare.

"I'm ready to get back into conference play," expressed State head coach Norman Sloan. "Conference games are so important to us."

While State's first half surge hardly broke a sweat, it was apparent that their sticky defense hardly gave Davidson an opportunity to shoot a high percentage shot.

"We could have done a lot better," said Wildcat senior Mike Sorrentino. "We got away too much from our regular game. We're at a point in the season where we're just not playing well."

Davidson travelled to South Bend, IN, a few weeks ago only to fall to the third-ranked Irish, 95–84. Sorrentino views the Pack somewhat on even terms with Notre Dame.

"If those two teams got together, it would be a heck of a game," noted the New York City native. "I felt a little more pressure playing at Notre Dame because it's a little different than playing on courts you become accustomed to like Reynolds Coliseum."

Sorrentino viewed individual matchups between Notre Dame and State as being vital to the outcome of the contest. "(Monte) Towe and (Dwight) Clay (a Notre Dame guard) are classy ballplayers, but Towe is quicker and probably a better shooter," stated the veteran guard.

Although Tommy Burleson only played 22 minutes, he accounted for 13 points, pulled down 7 rebounds, and rejected an occasional shot. Despite these contributions, Sorrentino was not satisfied.

"(John) Shumate (Notre Dame's starting center), from what I saw, is much better than Burleson," he said. "He is more of a complete player.

"Yet Notre Dame doesn't have a superstar like (David) Thompson," he added. "He would be the determining factor in a contest."

In getting back to the Wolfpack-Wildcat contest, Sorrentino, who scored 12 points in the game, felt the Wolfpack's quickness was vital in the decisive margin of victory (105–78).

"Towe was quick, but I think the team as a whole displayed quickness," he observed. "State has a lot more depth than us, and by this I mean quality depth."

State guard Moe Rivers and Towe were the 2 leading scorers for the Pack, contributing 24 and 17 points respectively. While the Davidson victory made it 23 straight home victories, the feat also brought about the 300th victory since Reynolds Coliseum was built in 1949.

Chapter 46

Wolfpack defeats Demon Deacons

From the Technician, February 18, 1974

By Jim Pomeranz

Sports Editor

State defeated conference foe Wake Forest, 111–96, Saturday afternoon in Reynolds Coliseum. Mark that win up as number 20 for the year out of 21 attempts for the high-geared Wolfpack.

Also, put that victory in the record book as the 24th straight win in Reynolds and as the 26th consecutive successful outing against opponents in the tough Atlantic Coast Conference. Duke owns the longest winning streak (28) over conference teams. That record was set in their 1963 and 1964 seasons.

But probably more important than those records is that the win over the Demon Deacons gives State a perfect 8–0 conference slate thus far this season.

And with only 4 more ACC regular season games remaining, the Wolfpack has the best chance of finishing first in the conference this year before heading into the ACC tournament. Carolina is the closest challenger with a 7–2 conference record.

"This is a big conference win for us," said Wolfpack head coach Norm Sloan after the game. "We now have 4 conference games left, and it's gonna be a dog fight all the way.

"It means a lot to us," he continued, "and we're not gonna get caught flat. You see what happened to Maryland at Clemson."

The Terrapins beat the Tigers Saturday, but only after Clemson held leads over Maryland, including a 1-point margin with only 35 seconds left on the clock.

The Pack's win over Wake Forest saw 5 State players scoring in double figures. All-American David Thompson was his usual self as he tossed in 31 points, and 7'4" Tom Burleson scored 26 points while playing as if he were completely at ease with the world. Both high leapers pulled a dozen rebounds each.

Junior guard Morris Rivers scored 19 points for the Wolfpack while Monte Towe and Tim Stoddard each added 11 for State.

Stoddard, while starting the year on a slow note, has been a great asset in the last month for the Pack, and Sloan is very pleased about Stoddard's improving performances.

"Stoddard played a superb ball game," praised the 8th-year State mentor. "Thank goodness he's coming on strong."

Sloan thought State played a "fine game overall. I thought we played very well," he continued. "David, Tommy, Monte, all of them played a good game."

Chapter 47

Covering SPORTS: UCLA loses two

From the Technician, February 18, 1974

By Jim Pomeranz

Sports Editor

Wolfpack fans have been talking about State being number one in the nation in basketball for the past two years. But the problem with such a statement has been a team called UCLA.

But not anymore.

State fans rejoiced Friday and Saturday night when two of the most remarkable things happened. The mighty Bruins lost two straight games over the weekend, and now the Wolfpack is atop the college basketball world.

On Friday night, UCLA was upset by Oregon State, 61–57. After that game, Bruin head coach John Wooden announced that his team "lacks the killer instinct they have had for years." On Saturday night, the remarkable happened. The Bruins lost its second in a row. This time Oregon was the victor, 56–51.

Carolina coach Dean Smith and Maryland Coach Lefty Driesell knew what they were talking about when they announced that they were the ones voting for State in the coaches poll last week. And Wooden has now become a Wolfpack believer even though the Bruins defeated State in St. Louis by 18 points.

Before the Oregon game Saturday, he announced he would cast his vote for State this week for first place. His opinion was reaffirmed after the game with the Ducks.

* * * *

Television has really become and asset to college basketball.

Usually, State head coach Norm Sloan runs players in and out of games as fast as you can wink an eye. But Saturday against Wake Forest, five players played most of the game with only two other players playing more than 10 minutes.

"TV games spoil us," explained Sloan after the game. "We know that we will get 4 official time-outs during the game, so in the second half, we just call time-out to give our players a rest. Conference games are important to us, and these rests are helpful."

* * * *

Wake Forest head coach Carl Tacy is much impressed with the performance of the State basketball team of late.

The Wolfpack defeated the Demon Deacons in the Big Four Tournament in Greensboro during the early part of January, and Tacy sees improvement.

"They (State) are better than earlier in the year," said the second year Deacon head coach. "The players have a lot more confidence. They are shooting better and running better. They run so fast that you could catch pneumonia on those fast breaks."

Chapter 48

Wolfpack is number one

From the Technician, February 20, 1974

By Jim Pomeranz

Sports Editor

Number one ranked and on top of the college basketball world. That's the Wolfpack basketball team. And thanks go out to the state of Oregon for providing the means.

Oregon State and Oregon universities both defeated UCLA last Friday and Saturday, and the Bruins were appropriately removed from their everlasting reign over basketball.

The United Press International and Associated Press wire services have both chosen State as the number one team in the nation this week, followed by Notre Dame as second and UCLA, third.

"We've been honored by being selected number one," said State head coach Norm Sloan.

However, some people around the nation, including Notre Dame coach Digger Phelps, have different opinions, but Sloan feels voting for the Pack is justified.

"I think anybody voting for the Wolfpack and supporting them for the number one spot has a very strong position," he stated. "It's not that I don't think other teams shouldn't be considered, and I can understand somebody supporting Notre Dame. I can understand somebody still supporting UCLA and also voting for teams like Pittsburgh and Vanderbilt.

"But I think those supporters of the Wolfpack have a strong argument in that we have played some of the strongest teams in the nation, including two of the top five teams on their home court, and defeated them. We beat Purdue when they were number one in the Big Ten, and we played them on their home court. We've played Furman, who has locked up the Southern Conference championship, on a neutral site, and had a fine game, and won that one by a large margin," Sloan continued.

"And we are undefeated in the very tough ACC," he emphasized, "so I think those people supporting us have a good position. We are a much better basketball team than we were in December. We are at least 25% improved and are getting better every day."

As the Pack prepares for a tough conference game with the Duke Blue Devils tonight, one may wonder if the top ranking will have any effect on State's basketball club. Will it help or will it hurt the Pack? And is it going to have any effect on the opposing teams in inspiring them to greater heights to defeat State?

"I don't think so," stated Sloan. "I think the fact they we have been undefeated for two years to this point in conference play is all the incentive that conference teams need to really get up for us. I think it should be a help to us. I think we should work a little harder and fight just a little bit more now to protect our being number one and prove that we deserve it."

State defeated the Blue Devils in Cameron Indoor Stadium in the two team's last meeting, 92–78.

Duke, under first year head coach Neil McGeachy, has compiled a 10–11 record thus far this year. The Blue Devils defeated Georgia Tech in their last outing.

Freshman Edgar Burch and junior Bob Fleischer have been the strong points in Duke's lineup thus far this season. At 6'8", Fleischer is on the small side for a center in the ACC but has performed well at that spot. Burch, a guard, started off the year on the bench, but he came on strong in mid-January and has gained a starting berth.

The Wolfpack's matchup with the Blue Devils will get underway at 8 p.m. and will be preceded by the intramural fraternity championship at 6:15.

Polls place State on top

The top ten college basketball teams in the nation as reported by the United Press International this week are as follows, with first-place votes and current record in parentheses:

1 .**NC State** (22) (20–1) 334

2. Notre Dame (10) (20–1) 318

3. UCLA (4) (18–3) 286

4. North Carolina (18–3) 190

5. Vanderbilt (20–1) 173

6. Maryland (17–4)............................ 137

7. Marquette (19–3) 96

8. Pittsburgh (21–1) 88

9. Southern Cal (18–3) 62

10. Indiana (16–3) 55

The top ten college basketball teams in the nation as reported by the Associated Press this week are as follows, with first-place votes in parentheses:

1. **NC State** (30) 1,034

2. Notre Dame (22)...................... 1,018

3. UCLA (3) 842

4. Vanderbilt (1)............................... 698

5. Maryland....................................... 635

6. North Carolina 602

7. Pittsburgh 493

8. Alabama... 388

9. Marquette 379

10. Indiana 296

Chapter 49

Number one State streaks past Duke

Reprinted from the Technician, February 22, 1974

By Jim Pomeranz

Sports Editor

"We're playing better all the time," commented State head coach Norm Sloan after the number one ranked Wolfpack had disposed of challenger Duke, 113–87, Wednesday night in Reynolds Coliseum before a sellout crowd of 12,400.

Playing better! That's an understatement. Playing great is more like it. How else should the new number one team in the nation perform? Doesn't the nation's top ranking have any more effect on a basketball team than just "playing better?"

"We're very proud of it—being number one," continued Sloan. "It has had a very positive effect. It might have been David's (Thompson) cause tonight. He was particularly quick and effective."

The All-American dazzled fans with his long bombs, his short teasing shots, and his "dunks" on his way to scoring his varsity career's second highest total of 40 points. Thompson was all over the court against the Blue Devils as he scooped up and down 14 rebounds.

"Tommy (Burleson) played good," the sharply dressed coach continued. "Timmy (Stoddard) performed well, and (Phil) Spence

156

came in and played well. I was real pleased with our performance. Number one does make a difference. It's a different feeling."

Duke coach Neil McGeachy had a similar reaction to the Wolfpack.

"NC State is definitely the top-ranked team in the country," praised the first year Blue Devil head coach. "We (Duke) applaud them."

McGeachy said that Thompson "may be the story in itself." His "40 points hurt us," he said. "Thompson is the best player in the nation.

"We lost to a better team with awesome talent," he continued. "When you play a team with the talent State has, any weakness you might have is magnified."

Duke thus far this season has played 5 teams ranked in the top 10 in the nation. Besides State, Carolina, and Maryland, the Blue Devils have met Pittsburgh and Notre Dame.

McGeachy thinks that a matchup between the Wolfpack and the Irish would be an interesting game.

"Notre Dame is a very fine team," he said. "But on the floor, State has 5 quicker players and overall, State's quickness is better. On the bench, State is stronger. They have 8 or 9 top players and are without a weakness. It's really hard to find a weakness in State.

"Sloan has done a fine job without a doubt," McGeachy praised. "I think State would beat them (Notre Dame) on a one-game basis."

McGeachy also noted that State has 2 of the best guards in Monte Towe and Mark Moeller.

"Towe is definitely first team All-ACC," he commented. "And some people talk about (Carolina's) Darrell Elston and others as underrated players. Well, I think Mark Moeller is THE underrated guard in the conference."

Burleson scored 17 points against Duke, Towe and Spence added 10, guard Morris Rivers 8, and Stoddard 6. Burleson collected 7 rebounds while Spence pulled down 13.

Saturday, the Wolfpack will travel to Clemson to take on the Tigers. Playing in the Tigers' Den is always a difficult task.

"Now we have to get ready to for Clemson," Sloan continued. "It's always a tough place to play. There's a lot at stake in this game. It's their (Tigers) biggest game because of our number one rating."

Chapter 50

Pray for Carolina; expect a State win

The Clemson game was played on a Thursday night, and the game story did not make it into the Friday, February 24 edition of the Technician and for good reason.

The game was a lot closer than the early January 96–68 win against the Tigers in Raleigh. With David Thompson playing the entire 40 minutes and scoring 35 points, and with Tommy Burleson knocking down 19 points and hauling in 10 rebounds, State won at Clemson, 80–75, after running up a 6-point lead in the first half.

Both teams shot better than 53% from the field. Both teams had 31 total rebounds. The difference was simply 1 more field goal and 3 more free throws made by the Wolfpack. As Sloan said a few days earlier, "It's always a tough place to play." It was, but the win moved State's record to 22–1 overall and 10–0 in the ACC.

Next up was a Tuesday night meeting with archrival North Carolina.

The reason the Clemson game results didn't make the paper, even the following Monday: The entire Monday, February 25 edition of the *Technician* was devoted to the home game with Carolina and the State basketball team.

One Carolina grad was firm about his heart and his head when it came to predicting the outcome of the next State-Carolina game.

United States Senator Sam Ervin, the face behind the Watergate hearings, came to the State campus on Monday, February 25, as a speaker in the "President and Congress in the '70s" symposium. Upon his arrival at the Raleigh-Durham Airport, he met briefly with three State student publications representatives. He answered questions with rapid fire and some humor.

When asked who would win the State-Carolina basketball game the next night, he stated, "Being a Carolina man, I'm going to pray for Carolina to win, but I'm going to expect State will."

Chapter 51

Carolina challenges number one State

Reprinted from the Technician, February 25, 1974

By Jim Pomeranz

Sports Editor

State vs. Carolina in anything means excitement, struggle, glamour, and sheer tough playing. Not only in one specific sport but in all sports is the before mentioned true.

But to a State or Carolina fan, a little more emphasis is placed on sports such as football and basketball. Last fall, State beat the Tar Heels in an exciting gridiron battle, and twice this basketball season, the same has been true.

The Wolfpack is definitely high on Carolina this year, and tomorrow night's battle with the fourth-ranked Tar Heels will be no different.

When the number one nationally ranked Wolfpack takes to the floor Tuesday at 9 p.m., State will be trying to defeat the Tar Heels for the seventh consecutive time.

Tar Heels' head coach Dean Smith's charges are led by Bobby Jones. The 6'9" senior has been the Tar Heels' strong point this season, averaging scoring in double figures, leading the team in rebounds and assists, and coming up with the right play at the right time.

Being in the right place was exemplified in Carolina's game against Duke earlier this year. Jones intercepted a pass, with 5 seconds remaining on the clock and the score tied, and raced to the basketball to score the game-winning points.

Smith has described the Charlotte native as "the complete player, who typifies our team concept of basketball." Jones was a preseason pick in *Street and Smith* magazine. Jones played on the 1972 Olympic team and helped lead that squad to the finals.

Backing up Jones is senior Darrell Elston, who many conference viewers consider one of the most underrated players in the ACC. The 6'4" guard is noted for his quickness and hustle.

Junior Ray Harrison, senior John O'Donnell, junior Ed Stahl, sophomore Mitch Kupchak, and super freshman Walter Davis make up the remainder of Carolina's starting seven players.

In the last meeting of these two high-powered teams, State handed the Tar Heels an 83–80 defeat in "Blue Heaven." In that game, State's All-American David Thompson tossed in 26 points to lead the Pack. Diminutive Monte Towe scored 21 points, and Tom Burleson added 14 points for State. The 7'4" center also pulled down 11 rebounds for the Pack. Phil Spence snared 10 loose balls for State that night.

After that game with State, Jones placed much emphasis on Thompson as the reason for State wins.

"Tonight, it was a one man thing," he said after that defeat. "Thompson is one of the greatest players I've ever seen. He just goes up and over you.

"It's really frustrating trying to guard Thompson," commented Jones, who had first crack at trying to counteract the play of the 6'4" guard-forward-center. "When he goes up for that jump shot, all you can do is put a hand in his face and hope he misses."

Jones says no one man can stop Thompson and even two may have trouble.

Jones says that there is only one way to beat State. "We can beat them with Thompson playing a good game, but not when he's awesome," he commented. "It would help if he had a bad game."

Chapter 52

Sloan: 'It all boils down to what the guys do on the court'

Reprinted from the Technician, February 25, 1974

By Bill Moss

Staff Writer

Norman Sloan stood in the midst of the 17 State basketball players, dwarfed by their size. "You guys are number one now, and you know what you have to do to protect it," he said.

He is a man who knows from 23 years of experience that too much coaching is not good coaching.

"I think some coaches tend to lead the public to believe that they have control over what's happening out on the court," he said as he watched his team practice. "It all boils down to what these guys do out on the court. The biggest mistake in coaching is over coaching."

Monte Towe, the team's leader out on the court, believes in Sloan's coaching style.

"He spends a lot of time with us individually, and he keeps us together as a unit," said the little man as he watched the coach working with Tommy Burleson. "Coach Sloan lets us play playground basketball. Too many X's and O's takes the fun out of it. The secret to his success is that he uses his talent to the fullest."

Success, though, for Norman Sloan is nothing new. The 47-year-old Indiana native has been named coach of the year in 3 major

164

conferences, receiving that honor twice in the ACC. His record in 7 years at State is 117–70, and twice he has coached State teams to ACC titles.

With Sloan, basketball has become a family affair. His son Mike is the team manager, and his wife Jo Ann sings the anthem at games.

"I'm particularly lucky because everyone in our family likes basketball," said the mentor. "We do get excited and enthusiastic over a big game, but we try to keep tenseness out of our house at all times."

Sloan also enjoys the team's ranking. "These are the happiest years we've had professionally," he commented. "Some people think there is a lot of pressure over having a great team, but it's just the opposite."

Sloan first came to State as a player during the Everett Case era. During his playing days, the Wolfpack won 3 conference titles and participated in 2 National Invitation Tournaments. Back in those days, State was the ACC king.

Norman Sloan returned to Raleigh in 1966, and once again, State reigns over the ACC.

Chapter 53

David Thompson is no 'Superman'

Reprinted from the Technician, February 25, 1974

By Jeff Watkins

Associate Editor

David Thompson is not faster than a speeding bullet, and he cannot leap tall buildings at a single bound—repeat—he cannot leap tall buildings at a single bound. With a running jump, all bets are off.

The junior from Shelby is about as close to Superman as you can get. He's everybody's All-American. He leads the conference in scoring for the second straight year, and his 666 points last year made him the highest scoring sophomore in State's history. And don't forget the World University Games in Moscow last summer when Thompson led the team in scoring (21-point average) and was instrumental in the defeat over the Russians in the championship game that helped the United States atone for the United States' basketball defeat during the '72 Olympics in Munich.

On the wall in Thompson's room, which he shares with Jerry Hunt, is a poster from the Moscow games signed by every member of the USA contingent; Kevin Stacom, Providence, "Stake and Brew;" Maurice Lucas, Marquette, "Sweet Black;" Wally Walker, Virginia, "The Wonder;" Marvin Barnes, Providence, "Bad News;"

Mitchell Kupchak, North Carolina, "Dr. K;" Tommy Burleson, "teammate," to name a few. The Atlantic Coast Conference was well represented at the games.

Talking about the players among the different conference teams, Thompson said, "Most of them seem pretty friendly off the court. There's still that rivalry on the court. I think it's good that the players can still be friends off the court.

"I know a lot of guys on the other teams. Wally Walker's a good friend. We became pretty close during the summer at the World University Games. We write every once in a while. Every time we play up there (Charlottesville), or they come down here, we talk a lot before and after the game."

Despite the fact that the Wolfpack was ranked first in both wire service polls last week, Thompson realizes that the most important goal lies ahead, and no votes are going to decide it.

It's a really good feeling," he said about the achievement. "It's not that different from being number two. We've still got a long season ahead of us. We want to be number one at the end of the year. That's the main thing."

Practice before the Duke game was short and informal. For the middling crowd of spectators who watched the goings-on, Thompson and Monte Towe put on their best show, matching each other in a half-court battle. In the un-officiated contest, both were pushing and shoving more than was allowable under game conditions. Shots were put up from various angles, like blind men simply going for broke.

Towe snagged a rebound and retreated to the free throw stripe. He pivoted and headed for the basket with Thompson in pursuit. He tossed the ball up a foot in front of the basket. Thompson leaped high in the air and slammed the ball against the backboard. The ball came off the glass and sailed over the 3-point line and bounced out of bounds.

Thompson came to State in the fall of 1971 from Crest High School in Shelby following a fierce recruiting battle. As a freshman, he was quiet and reserved, patiently waiting for football season to end so basketball could begin.

"I think I've become more mature as a person and as a ballplayer," he said. "I've learned to get along with people a lot better. I've never really had problems with that anyway."

It would be an understatement to say that David has received plenty of attention since he first stepped into his Sullivan dorm habitat over two years ago, be he hasn't changed.

"I'm the same person. I try to be the same person. I don't do anything special to keep it from going to my head. I guess I won't really know how important it is until I look back over it when I get older."

The game continues; all rules thrown out the window. Thompson drives on Towe and goes in for a layup. The ball rolls along the base of the rim and falls off. Certainly a rare miss, but then it's not often the defender grabs the back of the jersey and attempts to keep Thompson's feet on the ground, smiling the whole time.

Towe is not yet through with his taller opponent. He takes the ball, fakes out Thompson and goes in for a layup. David jumps for the block, and his swipe of the arm draws only air. The ball sinks through the basket.

Thompson is the youngest of 11 children. He learned the game on the playgrounds of Shelby, and whatever conditions enabled him to develop into one of the best collegiate stars in the country also worked on his roommate Hunt, who hails from the same city.

"There are a lot of recreation centers and parks around the area," he said. "Before four or five years ago, basketball was just about the only thing the kids played, because they didn't have any little league football teams or baseball teams. By playing basketball, I guess a lot of people became more talented."

Thompson listed some of the area stars who went on to bigger and better playgrounds, like Tony Byers of Wake Forest, Otis Cole of Florida State, George Adams, who played high school ball in Kings Mountain and is now with San Diego of the ABA, and Artis Gilmore, Gardner Webb, a product now with the Kentucky Colonels.

"A lot of times these people would go to the recreation centers and play with the kids," Thompson added.

David gets the ball back at midcourt with Towe guarding him closely. Revenge is quick this time. Thompson steps inside the 3-point line and guns over the small guard. His aim is true as the ball touches only the net on the way down.

Now on defense, Thompson grabs Towe from behind in a bear hug. The guard breaks free, however, and scores on a layup. Thompson strikes back almost immediately as both players begin trading baskets.

Since losing to UCLA in December, the Pack has reeled off 20 consecutive victories, including road victories over Carolina and Maryland. Thompson has seen improvement in the team since St. Louis.

"We're playing more as a unit. At the time we played UCLA, we were playing more as individuals, and everybody wanted to do their thing. We're playing good defense."

Last year's team, which compiled a 27–0 record, had an early season schedule that would make a Carolina's Conference school look good, much less a national contender. But with the Bruins on the schedule this year, things were quite different.

"We played some easier teams, and then we got to the tougher teams after we had gotten it together a little better. This year, we played UCLA in our third game; we weren't at our best."

The only rule in the one-on-one match was the offensive player had to shoot the ball when the opponent counted to three. Returning to the spot where he hits his long jumper, Thompson eyed the basket as Towe counted swiftly, "One-two-three." David jumped and shot, but immediately, one could tell the attempt was off. The ball traveled in a low arc and hit squarely in the corner between the rim and the glass, bounding back into Towe's grasp. Thompson faked a pout, saying, "My time's faster than yours." The team members sitting alongside the court laughed.

Thompson is a sociology major. Everyone takes for granted that pro basketball is in his future. What few people might know, however, is that he one day wants to have his own playground where future David Thompsons might learn to play.

"I'd like to start a recreation center of my own and have different types of events there, like dances and stuff like that. But in the daytime, have basketball clinics, working with kids, all kinds of kids."

The game was over, with no winner declared in the shootout. Thompson and (Morris) Rivers sat on the visitor's bench, laughing and throwing balls at the basket, never hitting but coming incredibly close. David got up to chase down a loose ball. He looked at the writer sitting under the basket and asked, "You want to talk now?"

Chapter 54

Towe: Maravich, Hawkins top guard's idol list

Reprinted from the Technician, February 25, 1974

[Note: The following is an interview with State guard Monte Towe after a short workout in Reynolds Coliseum Thursday before the away Clemson game. Towe measures 5'7" tall, weighs only 150 pounds, and hails from Converse, Indiana. He was not recruited by the Wolfpack but on the advice of Dick Dickey, former All-American under Everett Case. State took a chance on the small player. He is the smallest player ever to receive a basketball scholarship from State. Towe is presently second in field goal shooting percentage in the ACC behind Carolina's Bobby Jones. Most of Towe's shots are from way downtown, though, while Jones scores the majority of his on layups. Towe is averaging 13.2 points per game.]

JIM POMERANZ: Monte, when can you first remember that you started playing basketball and where?

MONTE TOWE: I can't remember anything over a week, but probably when I was about four years old. I had an older brother about three years older than myself. At that time, he was four and three; that makes him seven. He was just starting to play a little bit, and you know how you follow your big brother around a lot. At home is where I guess I started. I've got a big court at home on the side of the garage, and there is a pretty big area to play in

POMERANZ: Aside from sports, what is it you like to do?

TOWE: I'm pretty simple, really. I like to play basketball, and I enjoy college life. Whatever you call college life, I enjoy that. I like music quite a bit. It kind of relaxes me quite a bit. It just depends on what kind of mood I'm in as to what group I like to listen to. When I feel depressed, I listen to Cat Stevens a little bit. I like to listen to David Bowie. I like his lyrics. David Bowie is more rock 'n roll; Cat Stevens is a little softer. I like Elton John quite a bit. I think Rod Stewart is awfully good. And probably my favorite is the Rolling Stones. I guess I've got to say them because I like Jagger.

POMERANZ: Do you go to the movies much?

TOWE: Not by myself. Naw, I'm not a movie fanatic, but I do like good movies. I really don't do much. It's kind of funny. I think everybody expects us to be a little bit...you know, sometimes little kids think we're superhuman or something like that. They have trouble identifying us. Really, we do nothing spectacular. We just like to play basketball. I don't really study that much. I don't read that much, but I do enough to keep me educated, I think, and I know what's going on.

POMERANZ: Who would you say has had the greatest influence on your life?

TOWE: Greg Hawkins, I think. Hawk's been an inspiration to me because he's just so funny sometimes. Naw, I'd say Hawk's my idol probably. I can't say that much about Hawk because there is not that much to say about Hawk. On the serious side, I guess Pete Maravich.

Not my influence, but he's my idol. Hawk rates a close second hand, I guess.

POMERANZ: Why are you so short?

TOWE: I don't know. I only had one mother, I guess. That's one good reason. Some of the other guys had two or three. Naw, my parents are small and heritage, I guess. I didn't smoke when I was young, so I didn't stunt my growth.

POMERANZ: What do you generally do after basketball games?

TOWE: I like to be with the team. I think we all enjoy being with each other and talking about the game. I don't enjoy talking with other people after and about the game, but I enjoy being with my teammates and just associating with them. Sometimes we go to Bart's—you know, Pizza Bella—and we always gather there and talk about the game a little and have a good time. Again, nothing special. I like to relax and take it easy. I find myself more relaxed and being able to take it easy better when I'm with my teammates. They're the closest people I know here, and really, we're a close-knit group. We enjoy being around each other. It's just a close team.

POMERANZ: Do you enjoy traveling or visiting places other than Raleigh or home?

TOWE: I like Raleigh really well. When I leave this place, I feel like I'm leaving home. I stayed down here all last summer, and it's now my third year here in school. When we went to Purdue, everybody said, "Monte, you're going home." I felt like I was leaving home. I don't know that many people (in Converse, IN) anymore. I see my parents more than I do anybody else. They're about the only people I really have close contact with up there anymore plus my relatives. I like

Raleigh real well, but I do like to travel. During the summer, I go to a lot of basketball camps and work with a lot of kids, plus I get to see a lot of places in North Carolina. I'm not that familiar with the state because I haven't lived here but for three years. I'd like to do a lot more traveling after I get out of school. I think that one of my ambitions is to see the country a little bit. I've led a sheltered life. I've seen a lot of places that some people will never see, but there's still a lot of places I'd like to see.

POMERANZ: What is it you like about working with kids?

TOWE: I guess it's the innocence of youth. They seem to be openmouthed, expressive when you do something. And they're awed when you're sitting there talking. They're really taking in deep everything you say. There's no doubt in their minds. Like I said, they're innocent. I guess they enjoy what they are doing. It seems like when you get older, you stop enjoying life a little bit. I hope I never get to that point when I stop enjoying what I'm doing or enjoying anything. It's just that they have a good time out there. They're all eager, and they all want to learn. And for the most part, they are willing to work with you whatever you want them to do.

POMERANZ: Do you think there is a pro career in your future?

TOWE: I'm not even thinking about a pro career. I've got another year and a half here at State. I've just got a lot of things to do in that next year and a half—for one graduate. I think there's certain limitations. There's just too many good players night in and night out in the pros, I think. I really don't know how good I am. I play with a bunch of awfully good players. I think I may be overrated because they make me look better than what I am. As far as a pro career, I don't have any plans at all. I don't know what I'm going to do. I think about

174

coaching. Of course there's the traveling I like to do. There's a lot of things I hope will be open for me when I graduate. But really, I haven't thought about it that much because I'm caught up in what we are doing here.

POMERANZ: What is your major?

TOWE: I'm in sociology, liberal arts–sociology.

POMERANZ: Why did you decide on sociology?

TOWE: I like sociology. It deals with people, and it's not the psychic thing like psychology where you get into people's minds, although if I had more time, I might want to get into that. It's easier for me to relate to instead of a bunch of numbers and things like that. Other people can get into numbers—economics, or math, or chemistry. I would just rather read about people, and study people a little bit, and work on human behavior, and just general things you need to know about life.

Chapter 55

Almost Heaven: Nuce spurns WVa for State

Reprinted from the Technician, February 25, 1974

By Bill Moss

Staff Writer

It is a tight ACC basketball game, and Steve Nuce comes off the bench to give Tommy Burleson a rest.

The Pack comes down the court on offense, and Monte Towe, unable to get the ball inside, goes to Nuce in the corner. The 6'8" forward jumps and releases the ball from 20 feet away—swish.

Such is the value of Steve Nuce, a senior from Rockville, Maryland. When the going gets rough, he is one of several reserves who can be counted on to give the team a boost.

Nuce started playing organized basketball in the seventh grade, and he shows no sign of letting up. He didn't always pop those shots from the outside though. "I started playing on a church team in seventh grade," he said. "Believe it or not, I never shot. I was afraid to shoot the ball."

Obviously, Nuce's fear of shooting the ball was short lived. Attending the same high school as Paul Coder, he averaged 17 points per game as a sophomore guard (yes, that's right, guard). In his junior year of high school, Nuce moved to forward and scored 18 points per contest. His 27-point average in his senior year was enough to help him earn All-Metropolitan (DC) honors.

Nuce was contacted by over 150 schools who wanted his basketball services.

"About eight schools came after me really heavy," he recalled. "My parents went to West Virginia, and they wanted me to go there, but they were liberal enough to let me make my own decision."

This is not to say that his parents did not try to sway him. Nuce turned down his mother's offer to buy him a car if he went to West Virginia, and to Wolfpack country he came.

When Nuce came to Raleigh, State was not a national basketball power, but now the Pack is number one, and yes, there is quite a difference.

"Being number one brings so much attention to you," said the economics major. "Little kids want your autograph, and they can get on your nerves. That's just the price you have to pay."

Occasionally, Nuce and his friends forget basketball and take to the water. "Steve Smith has a boat, so when it's warm, we go out to Lake Wheeler and go skiing," he said. Then he added with a smile, "We taught Burleson how to ski, and he's really good now."

For Nuce, waterskiing is leisure fun, but basketball is still his life. "I'm constantly thinking about the team and basketball," he said. "I usually don't know what games are coming up, but I always think about it. It means a lot to me."

As basketball means a lot to Steve Nuce, Steve Nuce means a lot to basketball at State.

Chapter 56

Rivers fills gap in Wolfpack's lineup

Reprinted from the Technician, February 25, 1974

By Jim Pomeranz

Sports Editor

New York City is the basketball player capital of the USA. Think of that giant metropolis and the basketball products from there, and you probably think of Julius Irving, Charlie Scott, Kareem Abdul Jabar, and John Roche.

But now there is one more name to add to the list.

Morris Rivers, a Brooklyn, New York, native, stepped onto the State campus last fall and found a void in the starting lineup of the number two nationally ranked Wolfpack.

Rivers came to State from Gulf Coast Junior College where he was an All-American and Conference Player of the Year.

In NYC, like most of those well-known players from there, Rivers started playing at an early age.

"I've been playing for ten years," said the 21-year-old junior. "I first got started playing in Catholic League with a Catholic Church in the area." Rivers, though, did not just play basketball.

"When you're young, you've got three or four different sports you might be interested in," stated Rivers. "I was playing baseball as well as trying to play a little football. As I kept playing basketball, I found out it attracted my interest, so I stuck with that—playing ball."

And "ball" it has been and is for the 6'1" guard. He played in summer leagues before high school, and then he broke it open his senior year. Rivers averaged 20.2 points per game that year on the New York City champion George Wingate High team. He was then named to the all-city team for his performance in that 18–0 year.

Morris is right when he remarked, "It's almost every ball player's goal to try to play for a college team or even go pro." Rivers wanted to play in the Atlantic Coast Conference, but grade difficulty kept him out.

"During my last year in high school, I did rather well, and I was receiving offers from all over the country and from junior colleges as well too," he explained. "I had narrowed down my offers to come to State, Maryland, or Wake Forest. I didn't have time to take the SAT again, so I picked a junior college."

While in Florida, Rivers had visited Gulf Coast and had liked it so much that he decided to go there for two years.

Like many players, Rivers wanted to play in the ACC because of the competitiveness and the area.

"I feel to reach my goal, I would have to play in the conference with the best to get to see how good I am or how much I can excel," said Morris. "And the ACC happened to be one of the toughest conferences in the country. Also, the fact that it was on the Atlantic coast, and I wanted to stay in my native area, so to speak. And as I heard about the ACC, it increased my values for wanting to be a part of it."

Rivers said that it took some time to get adjusted to the environment of the big campus life, but he adjusted very well. He commented that his social life has been nice, but that was not his primary goal at State.

"You see," he said, "my social life is what I'm gonna make it anyway. My main interest is playing ball and getting my degree."

His degree will be in industrial education, but his interest in the off-season is one of fun and relaxation. He plays basketball almost year-round except for one month in the summer in which he does not touch a roundball.

"I just like to take a little time out to just enjoy myself and enjoy life," the easygoing Rivers said. "I just like to relax. Wherever there are concerts, I like to be there. I enjoy music and rock groups, and I enjoy rapping with people.

"I like to travel," he continued. "I think that's what I'm going to do in the off season. I was down in Florida for two years, and I enjoyed that during that time. Florida is pretty good during the summer and, as a matter of fact, all year round. I might go down there for a week or two this year."

Morris Rivers is a true basketball player. His moves on the court astonish fans as well as opposing players. He handles the ball like a great magician performs tricks.

New York City and NC State should both be proud to claim him.

Chapter 57

Tommy, State adjust to changes

Reprinted from the Technician, February 25, 1974

By Jim Pomeranz

Sports Editor

Call him Tall. Call him Tommy. Call him Burleson. Call him any number of descriptive terms, but he is still one of the most dominating figures in basketball today.

And he is also one of the most dominating figures to play basketball in the history of the roundball sport since the first peach basket was attached to a wall 10 feet off the ground.

Tommy Loren Burleson came to State in the summer of 1970 from the mountain county of Avery. Not only did he have to adjust to the new atmosphere to which he had been introduced, but the university had to make a few changes itself to accommodate the 7'4" Newland native.

Even before he stepped on the campus and donned a State uniform, preparations were made in a dorm room in Burgaw Residence Hall to take in the tremendous body frame of Burleson.

A student that summer told the story that he was taking a nap one day when all of a sudden, two men entered the room and asked that he move to the other bed. Without question, the puzzled lad changed beds, and, to his amazement, his bed was removed and another was

181

put into its place. It was, though, no ordinary bed. Its length was just long enough to handle about seven and a half feet worth of basketball player.

Burleson's 7'4" has posed no major problems for the tallest basketball player in the nation. As a matter of fact, he sort of enjoys it.

"I can be seen," said Burleson. "I stand out in a crowd, and people can recognize me easily. I like it."

"Standing out in a crowd" is an understatement if there ever is such a thing. This dominating structure has to stoop to great lengths just to enter doors and when walking past ceiling light fixtures in hallways.

"There is no problem (being 7'4")," he continued, "just advantages. It gives me an advantage on the basketball court and in life." Burleson loves to be able to be noticed, and that is no problem.

Burleson explains that his ability to be playing college basketball was dependent on his height.

"If I was 6'8" or under, being from Avery County, I probably wouldn't have been given the chance to play basketball at all," he said.

"Avery County is like a foreign country to many people in this area. Hell, it's almost in Tennessee. But the activity there is much like the fun students have in their respective town or county. Excitement is … well … er … excitement.

"You get your car," told Burleson about all the excitement of Newland, "and fix it up. Then you drive it around the local snack bar, or whatever.

"But very little is going on as far as sports play such as big parks where people can get out and go," he said.

But Burleson played sports in Newland, and that, along with of course his moving 7'4" body, helped him get a scholarship to play basketball at State. And he has done quite a bit of that in the last four years. He was fourth in ACC scoring during the Pack's 27–0 season last year and led all rebounders with a 12.0 average. His performance in the ACC tournament won him the Everett Case Award for outstanding play.

Burleson was a member of the 1972 United States Olympic team and a teammate of David Thompson on the United States University World Games team.

But there is plenty of basketball left in the senior's life, and he knows it.

"My career is sort of predestined as it is to a professional basketball player," Tommy established. "And I feel when basketball is over for me—five to eight years from now—I would fall back onto my education at State." Burleson is studying business administration.

Burleson is a real asset to the State basketball team, and State is lucky to have him, and he likes being at State.

"That's (the atmosphere) one of the reasons I came to State," he explained. "The people were so nice, and the campus is really beautiful because of its modern architecture. But I still like to go back to Avery County and get out in the country and go horseback riding."

And the likeable fellow is sincere when he said he liked modern architecture.

"Yes," he sharply stated. "I prefer it over Chapel Hill."

Chapter 58

Covering SPORTS: Interesting game facts

Reprinted from the Technician, February 25, 1974

By Jim Pomeranz

Sports Editor

During the 1963 and 1964 Duke basketball seasons, the Blue Devils won 28 consecutive ACC basketball games. Their next opponent was Carolina, and they lost.

State has now won 28 consecutive ACC basketball games, and, you guessed it, the Wolfpack takes on Carolina tomorrow night.

In 1959, State gained the number one ranking around mid-season. Eight days later, State was defeated by Carolina. Tomorrow night, about eight days after the top ranking was bestowed upon the Wolfpack, you guessed it, the Wolfpack takes on Carolina.

Not wanting to bestow a bad omen on tomorrow night's clash with our sister institution, I thought the above information might be interesting to today's readers.

For the past four years, State has played Carolina in basketball 12 times, and the Wolfpack has come out on top in 7 of those outings.

For the past 6 State-Carolina games, the Wolfpack has been the victor, and a win tomorrow will not only extend that streak to 7, but it will increase the Wolfpack's ACC victory streak to 29 and place State in a strong grip of the number one national ranking.

Chapter 59

Moeller: Ohioan almost passed up 'big time'

Reprinted from the Technician, February 25, 1974

By Ray Deltz

Staff Writer

"We are able to function effectively as a team because we can play 8 or 9 players without any hesitancy," remarked coach Noam Sloan in regard to his no. 1-ranked Wolfpack squad. "Mark Moeller fits in this category."

To the average fan, Moeller might be considered State's third guard. Yet, few opponents of State find the going any easier when Moeller checks into the lineup to give Monte Towe or Morris Rivers a rest.

"I feel my job is to keep things going at the same pace when Monte or Morris goes out," said the Wolfpack guard. "With the type of game we play, it's essential to utilize 8 or 9 players."

Moeller, an Ohio native, almost never made it south. "I was all set to sign with a small school in Ohio when Eddie (Biedenbach, Wolfpack assistant coach) mentioned to some administrators at a basketball camp that he needed a guard. Craig (Kuszmaul, Wolfpack guard) and I were working at the camp at the time," reflected Moeller. "I jumped at the opportunity. I wanted to go to a big school that had a big-time basketball reputation.

"Up in Ohio, I followed the Big Ten pretty much when I was in high school," continued the junior guard. "But I would always hear about fights in the ACC and knew it was a great basketball league. I'd see teams in the national rankings every year in the ACC."

Long Beach State is the latest in a long line of schools to be put on probation because of alleged recruiting violations. Although Moeller views recruiting as a tricky business, he felt that successful recruiting will often put a town on the map.

"When a kid makes up his mind to go to a particular school, he's got to believe in what the coaches say. It's a rough deal," he said. "Yet, it's one of the most important parts of college sports. Look at what it did to Jacksonville with Artis Gilmore. But any way you look at it, it can be rough on the kid and on the school."

Even if State had a junior varsity basketball program, it is hardly conceivable that Sloan would relegate a valuable tool such as Moeller to such a team. Sloan viewed the program as being nonessential to the development of future Wolfpack talent. "Coach Sloan felt that JV players would get just as much experience practicing with the varsity," stated Moeller.

Although the Pack has one more loss than last year at this juncture in the season, it seems pretty obvious that this season's edition is stronger and better balanced than the 27–0 squad.

"We seem to be running a little more than last year and double-teaming more in the backcourt," expressed the steady guard. "Some of us worked in basketball camps over the summer, Tim (Stoddard) played baseball, and David (Thompson) and Tommy (Burleson) played in the World Games. So I think we're stronger than last season. Also, I feel that there is a lot of unity on this squad, which is a key to success."

What's Mark Moeller's biggest thrill to date as a Wolfpack player?

"Winning the ACC championship last season," he said. "I hope to have the biggest one this season (the NCAA championship). It's just a thrill to be playing with the no. 1 team."

Mark Moeller never makes the headline in the sports section. Nor does he register a bulging point total in the scoring column. Yet without his calm, consistent play, State's quality depth could be dealt a severe blow.

Chapter 60

Hawkins has own style

Reprinted from the Technician, February 25, 1974

By Jim Pomeranz

Sports Editor

Greg Hawkins is a cool guy. He's got to be. To begin with, the "Hawk" is Monte Towe's idol. What more could anyone ask?

As a senior, Hawkins is only in his second year as a Wolfpack basketball player. He transferred from Tennessee to State in the fall of 1971. The move was something that Hawkins really wanted.

"I wanted to play on a better team," said the 6'5" guard-forward, "and on a team that was ranked high and would have a chance of doing well. As you can see, we're number one in the country.

"Also, it was a different kind of ball at Tennessee," he continued. "I wanted to play more my style, like I did in high school. In Tennessee, we went over there, and they tried to change us a lot. They tried to slow us down some. It's not that way anymore. They're changing their ways at Tennessee now even.

"I also knew about Burleson," Hawkins confessed. "And it just looked good. I wanted to be in the ACC."

Hawkins mentioned something about wanting to play more his style. Well he's definitely got a style all his own. Not only on the court—where that style gained him the first Ken-L-Ration award given at State last year—does he have that special style, but off the playing surface as well, now and throughout most of his life.

Just ask him sometime about doing things when he wants to do something, and Hawkins will probably tell you he's "pretty independent," and that he is.

"I'm not afraid to do anything, really," stated the Huntington, West Virginia, native. "I just go out and do it. I take off, and I hitchhike to the beach if I want to. Or, I take off and hitchhike to St. Louis. I did that one time.

"One summer, I was on my way home from basketball camp," he explained. "I got to Wheeling, West Virginia, and there was a guy going to St. Louis, so I just went with him. I didn't know him; I just hitchhiked.

"I like to do whatever I feel like doing," Hawkins stated. "I've been able to so far. Maybe things will change when I get out of college. Hopefully, I can go to Europe, and play a little basketball, and have pretty much the same life when I go there. I like to feel like I can do what I want to do."

Greg Hawkins is the "baby" of his family, or that is to say, he is the youngest of three children. As a kid, he was able to develop his athletic talents through many means, including neighborhood fights.

I played Biddy Basketball. I played little league baseball. I played midget league football. I played wiffle ball in the back yard," said Hawkins.

"We had gang wars. We had fights around the neighborhood. We had two armies, one on Edison Drive and one on Woodland Drive," he explained. "And we were tops because we had the tallest treehouse, and they couldn't get us. But we couldn't get them."

Now that's style.

Hawkins is very athletic minded and has been since that small age of eight when he first picked up a ball. His favorite sport in high school though was not basketball. He was one of the best football players in the state of West Virginia.

As a senior, he made the All-State pigskin team. He played tight end and defensive halfback. As a tight end, he caught 10 touchdown passes during that season, 3 in one game as he tells it. And on defense, he intercepted 10 aerials. Tennessee recruited him, though, to play basketball.

Chapter 61

Spence: JC transfer adds new dimension to Wolfpack

Reprinted from the Technician, February 25, 1974

By Steve Wheeler

Staff Writer

Phil Spence, a junior transfer, has added a certain dimension to the number one ranked Wolfpack this season in helping them to a 22–1 overall record and a 10–0 ACC slate.

Spence, a 6'8", 210-pound forward from Raleigh, has given State another big forward with good rebounding strength and speed. The big frontcourt man has averaged 6 points and 6 rebounds a game in a role of starting about half of the Pack's games and coming off the bench of late to add to the "Big Red Machine."

A sophomore, Spence has a philosophy about life that others should take note of. "I see life as a challenge in every way," he said. "I like to meet people, get to know them, and learn as much about them as I can. The reason I do this is because I'll be meeting people every day for the rest of my life, and if I can't get along with them, I won't make many friends, and that's what it is all about."

Just as Spence sees life as a challenge, he also sees being on the number one team in the nation as a major challenge. "We're number one right now, and I am very proud to be there. But, we cannot get cocky because everyone will be out to knock us off," stated Spence.

"It's a challenge to get to the top, and we've done that, but we'll have to play our best to stay there."

Among his other interests, Spence enjoys just being alone and listening to music. "Sometimes, I will just go to my room in my spare time and turn on the music. Then, I will lie down and try to find solutions to any problem I might have."

A sociology major, Spence also writes a lot of poetry. As he tells it, "It's just a way I've found to express myself to others. I just love to write."

When Spence entered State last fall, he was changed from center to forward, an unfamiliar position to him but a challenge.

"I did not mind moving to forward because coach Sloan is the coach," he continued, "and he knows best; you can tell by his record. Anywhere he wants me, I'll go." Spence's best performance of the season was probably last Wednesday night against Duke. The big forward came off the bench to score 10 points and snare 14 rebounds in only 15 minutes playing time."

Spence has certainly added a new dimension to the Wolfpack's play this year.

Chapter 62

After slow start, Stoddard regains form

Reprinted from the Technician, February 25, 1974

By Steve Wheeler

Staff Writer

After a rather slow start this season, Tim Stoddard has come around to play the sound kind of basketball that was expected of him after a steady sophomore year last year.

At 6'7", 225 pounds, Stoddard is a fierce competitor on the backboards and has a soft outside touch for a big man. In the last few games, Stoddard has found his shot from the perimeter and has been hitting.

When the season opened, Stoddard was being pressed hard for the big forward position by Phil Spence and Steve Nuce. He also came in overweight. But after getting down to size, Stoddard won back his starting nod over Spence, and both have been playing well since.

"I was playing kinda bad at the start of the season," the junior stated, "but I've gained my confidence back now. I am moving better without the ball, which has helped me tremendously."

During the halftime ceremonies of the Duke game last week, Stoddard was bestowed a big honor by being awarded the Case Athletic Scholarship for 1974. Stoddard, majoring in economics, said it was "a great privilege to be named" for the award." Stoddard also added, "I really feel good about the respect they (selection committee) gave me. They really made me feel good."

The Case Award is given to an outstanding basketball player each year by the athletics department. David Thompson, Tommy Burleson, and Monte Towe have been past recipients of the award.

Stoddard graduated in 1971 from Washington Senior High School in East Chicago, Indiana, as a standout student-athlete. The husky forward pulled in a total of 11 letters while in high school.

As a matter of fact, in his last four years, Stoddard has suffered just two losses in basketball, one in a freshman game to Carolina and one in the UCLA game this season.

As tournament time rolls around again, Stoddard will be counted on, as he was last year, to be a steady performer. In the final seconds of the ACC championship game against Maryland last year, Stoddard sank 2 big free throws to help ensure defeat for the Terrapins.

Stoddard is also playing varsity baseball at State and doing very well at it. Last season, the big hurler had a 4–0 record and a good earned run average.

But the overlapping of basketball and baseball seasons does not bother him.

"I've already started throwing and getting my arm back in shape," Stoddard said. "Of course, I hope we'll be playing basketball for a while longer, but when we get through, I'll be ready to start throwing hard."

So, after a slow start to his junior season, Tim Stoddard has come around to play the kind of basketball that was expected of him and is making a genuine contribution to the number one ranked Wolfpack.

Chapter 63

Kuszmaul's dedication is sign of future success

Reprinted from the Technician, February 27, 1974

By Steve Baker

Staff Writer

State guard Craig Kuszmaul came to North Carolina with the reputation of being quite an offensive threat. He achieved this reputation by holding all of his high school's scoring records but one. He missed the record for most points scored during his junior year by 5 points but finished his career in prep school with 1175 points, the closest challenger having only 825.

Offense, however, hasn't been Kuszmaul's main concern since donning the red and white of the Wolfpack. "I feel defense is my best friend," explained the 6'5" Warren, Ohio, native. "I think I can contain just about anyone in the conference."

Craig sites his emphasis on defense as one factor that determines the amount of playing time he sees. "We stress defense a lot, but I think we did more so last season," said Kuszmaul. "The fact that Tommy Burleson and David Thompson are there to back you up has enabled us to open up more.

"Also, our offense has been so effective this season; we haven't had to rely on a real tough defense quite as often. I think we'll be depending more on our defense next season with Tommy graduating, and I hope to see more action then," concluded the junior.

Limited playing time hasn't caused Kuszmaul to regret choosing State in the least bit. "I'm happy to be associated with guys like Monte Towe, Burleson, and Thompson, and I'm proud to be on the best team in the country," explained the industrial arts major. "I feel I'm making a contribution to the team, and I'll continue to do what I can to ensure team success.

"Basketball, however, wasn't my only reason for choosing State," continued Kuszmaul. "In picking a college, I was looking for one with a good industrial arts school, and State has just that. I'm really getting the education I wanted here."

Kuszmaul has set his goal in life and hopes to achieve it following graduation. "I would like to return to Ohio and teach industrial arts. Also, my father owns a building firm, and I hope to take over someday."

Basketballs aren't the only thing you'll find Kuszmaul shooting. "Hunting is my favorite pastime. I enjoy most any type of hunting and spend a lot of my spare time with my hunting companion in Cary."

Kuszmaul has equipped himself for this sport most adequately. At his home in Ohio, Craig has a gun collection, which he estimates is worth over $3,000. "I have several handguns and just about any type of rifle or shotgun you care to name," he explained. "I guess I could arm a small army. Hunting and gun collecting have always been part of my life."

Whether in the field or on the court, it is obvious that Craig Kuszmaul is not the type to go unprepared. His thoroughness and dedication to those things in which he becomes involved are sure signs of future success both in basketball and life.

Chapter 64

Johnson: Delaware State transfer came home to play

Reprinted from the Technician, February 13, 1974

By Steve Baker

Staff Writer

"Pistol Pete" Maravich was perhaps the best high school prospect ever produced in Raleigh. Not far behind, however, is State cager Dwight Johnson. Johnson, at the time of his high school graduation, was acclaimed by many knowledgeable sports writers as one of the top Raleigh products of all time.

Although he was a Raleigh native and Wolfpack fan, Johnson did not pick State initially as the school he would attend. Instead, he chose Delaware State. "I wanted to move away from home and live on my own for a while," explained the 6'0", 175-pound guard.

Johnson did well away from home, starting as a freshman for Delaware State and averaging 12 points a game. His stay in Delaware, however, was short and sweet.

Following his freshman season, Johnson decided to return to Raleigh and hopefully ACC competition. "I realized Delaware State wasn't what I wanted basketball-wise," he said. "So when I came home for Christmas, I contacted several schools to see if I could play ball for one of them."

Among the schools the sophomore contacted were Oklahoma, Maryland, Carolina, and State. Johnson managed to narrow his choice to Maryland or State, then after some careful thought and advice from State football star Willie Burden, he chose State.

"When I was in high school, I always thought I'd play for (Maryland coach Lefty) Driesell. He came and talked to me when I was just a sophomore. After Willie told me about the campus and people here at State, though, I changed my mind."

Johnson's final decision has proven to be a happy one for both him and the basketball program.

"Dwight is a fine athlete with a lot of ability," stated Wolfpack assistant coach Eddie Biedenbach. "He has a good attitude, works hard, and is well liked by all who know him. He helps set a good team image."

Johnson looks confidently at his contribution to the team. "When I get into a game, I try to see either that our team gains an advantage or at least remains even," he explained. "I don't want our opponent to gain an advantage when I'm in there."

Playing time has been limited for Johnson this season as well as for some of the other members of the squad. He is quick to point out, however, that playing in the game is not the only way he and the others contribute to a victory.

"The regulars have to have quality competition to practice against, and we supply that," stated the fiery guard. "We help them prepare, and they help us learn how to compete in the ACC. This team's got a great attitude, and every man has a job to do."

Wolfpack basketball has not been the only thing in Johnson's life since his return to Raleigh. The son of a Raleigh doctor and assistant State librarian, he has always had a desire to work with younger kids and feels that his basketball abilities have helped him to reach many of them.

"I barely got home from our Sugar Bowl games before a bunch of kids wanted me to come down to the mini-park and shoot a few with them," explained the liberal arts major rather happily. "I get to work with a lot of them this way.

"As far as my future, I hope I can continue to work with kids," Johnson said, "and maybe even do some coaching. I'd also like to continue my playing career after college, but that possibility remains to be seen."

Johnson's pro prospects may be uncertain at the moment, but his prospects for the next few seasons with the Wolfpack are much clearer.

"The ACC is a tough league and breaking into it is hard for a newcomer," explained Biedenbach. "Dwight's tough, though, and we'll be counting on him to help in the future."

Chapter 65

No. 1 subs explain roles

Reprinted from the Technician, February 25, 1974

By Louise Coleman

Staff Writer

There are only three minutes left in the game, and it's time-out State.

Norm Sloan glances down at his bench where he faces anticipation and eagerness in the eyes of his freshman players. He motions to them to substitute for the starting five.

How many freshmen players would enjoy the opportunity to guard or substitute for stars David Thompson, Tommy Burleson, and Monte Towe?

It's apparent that the deletion of the JV program from State basketball has proven to be a successful formula. As the number one team enters the homestretch of the season, the finest example of comradeship and friendship is evinced by the 12 upperclassmen and 5 freshmen of the Wolfpack.

Sloan's decision provoked skeptics into asking what kind of attitude would young players develop knowing they would see limited action.

Bruce Dayhuff, a freshman liberal arts business major, feels it is an advantage to play varsity ball rather than junior varsity because "it is

200

tougher competition, and it should make me a better ball player overall."

The Walkerton, IN, native played as both a guard and forward in high school and has seen more action in varsity games than the other freshmen.

"I am real glad to have had the opportunity as a freshman to see action," he stated. "I am really happy to play the part I do because I knew I would be into some tough competition when I came here."

Freshman Ken Gehring played the forward position. He concurs with Dayhuff that it is an advantage to play varsity ball.

"You get great experience," said the Akron, Ohio, native. "And you are playing with great players such as Thompson, Burleson, and Towe."

But as always, there is a big adjustment between high school basketball and the college ranks, and freshman Bill Lake thinks that one adjustment is in the size department.

"It's a big adjustment for me because I didn't play with guys my size in high school," said the 6'11" center. "Also there is a lot more individual thinking. Where you have to read your other players because everyone is so good, you have to work with them to understand what they are going to do."

Dayhuff also points out a difference in the prep level and the college level.

"They (the coaches) have their certain style of ball you have to conform to, but you still get to use your individual moves," explained the 6'2" guard. "I play more conservative ball here than I did in high school. I mainly freelanced there."

Dayhuff, Gehring, Lake (all freshmen), and sophomores Steve Smith and Jerry Hunt do not receive the publicity that the other 11 players do, but they are definitely a part of the number one team in the nation and an important part at that.

Their two or three remaining years on the Wolfpack basketball team will gain them the deserved spotlight, but for the time being, they add to State's roundball program on the practice court, on the playing court, and off the court through association with the rest of the team.

Lake summed up the feelings of not only the 6 players on the south end of the bench, but also of the remainder of the squad.

"We enjoy working together," he explained. "We are a close-knit group who seem to understand each other on the floor."

And that's where it counts.

Chapter 66

Burleson second half play sparks Pack

Reprinted from the Technician, March 1, 1974

By Bill Moss

Staff Writer

The skeptics who said State could not win the big ones unless David Thompson had a good game found themselves eating crow after the Wolfpack defeated Carolina, 83–72, Tuesday night.

Tommy Burleson and Morris Rivers were primarily responsible for serving the meal as they both hit 8 of 13 attempts from the floor, combining for 41 points.

The first half belonged to Rivers as he scored 12 points and had a couple of those lightening quick steals.

"I prepared myself for this game," said the slender guard after the contest. "I knew we could lockup first place in the conference, and I was up for this one. I just played my game, and as it turned out, I got off to a good start."

It was lucky for State that Rivers did have a good start. Burleson could only get 3 points in the first half and Bobby Jones' defense on David Thompson held him to 8 first half points.

It was Rivers' buckets from the outside that carried State in the beginning, but Burleson, playing inspired ball for the last 20 minutes, carried the Wolfpack in the end.

The senior pivotman played superbly in the second half, collecting 19 points and 9 rebounds.

"I just did something I have never done before. I gave Tommy Burleson the game ball," said coach Norm Sloan after his team clinched the ACC regular season title. "We're undefeated in this league over the last two years, and this big man is primarily responsible for it."

In the dressing room, a satisfied Burleson talked of his play in the game. "I was pressing too much in the first half because I was thinking about this being my last (regular season home) game," he said. "In the second half, I went out with a relaxed mind and concentrated on playing hard."

Steve Nuce, another senior playing his last home game at Reynolds Coliseum, praised the big man's play. "He ignited us when we were down," he said. "If Burleson plays the way he played tonight, we can dominate any game we play."

Monte Towe did not hit the 25 footers with his usual accuracy, and Thompson was held to 21 points, but Burleson and Rivers proved something Tuesday night. State is not a one-man team.

Chapter 67

Heels praise State's play

Reprinted from the Technician, March 1, 1974

By Ray Deltz

Staff Writer

In addition to being the Pack's seventh consecutive win over its neighboring institution, Tuesday night's victory over Carolina, 83–72, was the Pack's most decisive in the seven-game stretch. In coach Dean Smith's post-game interview, he might have made a few friends with hostile Wolfpack fans.

"Although I'll be pulling for us (Carolina) as much as ever in the ACC tournament, it would definitely be a shame if State doesn't go to the NCAAs," said Smith. "This is the best State team I've seen since I've been here, and I've been here a pretty long time.

"We had some moments in the game but not enough of them," said the highly successful coach. "We had trouble getting it inside. (Ed) Stahl had to put up the 20 footers."

Smith praised State's quickness, a quality he feels often goes undetected. "When people talk about State, too often they just talk about their size with (Tim) Stoddard, (Tommy) Burleson, and (Phil) Spence," he noted. "State also has so much quickness."

Walter Davis, one of the nation's top freshmen performers, collected 18 points and 8 rebounds in the Tar Heels' fourth loss of the season. The slender Charlotte native credited the Wolfpack with having a great team.

"Although Thompson didn't have one of his typical super games, he still did a great job," Davis reflected. "You have to always point to Burleson and Towe to come through.

"I would have liked to penetrate more, but State's defense held us off," added Davis.

Before the versatile freshman made his first visit to Reynolds Coliseum Tuesday night, he had heard bad stories about the place. "I kept hearing that people would always take swings at you at State," expressed Davis. "But playing at State is just like playing at any other coliseum on the road."

Darrell Elston, who always seems to sport his finest shooting touch against the Pack, wound up collecting 19 points. The Tar Heels guard praised the Wolfpack defense, which cut off Carolina's penetration.

"In the second half, it was much harder to make an assist inside. We wanted to go inside but had to go to the outside and thus ended up shooting only 43%," explained Elston. "On defense, I caught myself not boxing out enough."

Elston compared the superlative play of Tommy Burleson to that of UCLA's Bill Walton. "Burleson is a lot like Walton. If he's on, it's really hard to beat him," he said.

"I have seen a very noticeable improvement in State's play since the UCLA game," praised Elston. "But I still have confidence that we can beat them."

Chapter 68

Seniors lead basketball turnaround

Editorial reprinted from the Technician, March 1, 1974

The Wolfpack's win over Carolina Tuesday night showed ACC basketball fans more than just a good game. Besides claiming the first round bye in the upcoming ACC tournament next week, State set a record for most consecutive wins over conference foes, extended its winning streak over the Tar Heels to seven straight, and further, showed the nation that the Pack does indeed have a rightful claim to the top ranking in the nation.

Coach Norman Sloan and his crew have achieved their first major goal of the season, that of winning the ACC regular season championship. Next in their quest for the NCAA crown is the conference tournament, which gives them a spot in the Eastern Regional to be held in Reynolds Coliseum. At this time, we want to wish them added success in next week's tourney and also to acknowledge the seniors on the 1973–74 edition who played a vital part in achieving the coveted number one national ranking.

Since Tommy Burleson played his first varsity contest in a Wolfpack uniform, the basketball program has soared to heights unprecedented in State's history. He has developed his skills to such a degree as to warrant a position on the Olympic basketball squad and a spot on the World University Games championship basketball team. He has indeed attracted international attention to the State campus.

Steve Nuce, a senior from Rockville, MD, has also earned a spot in the Wolfpack basketball history book. Several times, he has come off the bench in place of Burleson, hit some clutch shots, and enabled the team to function smoothly despite missing the services of the 7'4" big man. Nuce as a starting forward or a reserve center has proved that he can be counted on.

Greg Hawkins, a transfer from Tennessee, has made hustle his trademark since coming to State. Recipient of the first Ken-L-Ration Award for his play, Hawkins has the habit of making things happen when he enters the contest. His desire is apparent from his style of play, and he has become a favorite of the fans who attend Wolfpack games.

When these three came to State, the basketball program was floundering. Playing .500 basketball, the team could rarely put a winning streak of any sort together. For the past two years, however, the Pack has amassed a 50–1 record, the best two-year record in modern times for any collegiate team.

Yes, when these three came to State, the team had no place to go but up. And when they walked off the court Tuesday night after their last regular season home game, they went out winners, and now the entire nation knows it.

Now, it's onto Greensboro for the championship of the Atlantic Coast Conference and eventually for the championship of the NCAA.

Chapter 69

The greatest game ever

Before the Wolfpack packed its bags for Greensboro for the ACC tournament, State had one more regular season game. It was a March 2 game at Wake Forest won by State, 72–63, but not covered by the *Technician* because of spring break. When the campus closed, the *Technician* did as well.

In the Wake Forest game, State led at the half, 45–35, and coasted to the final score. Thompson scored 21 points; Burleson had 17 points and 16 rebounds. The win pushed State's ACC mark to 12–0, far better than second place finishers Maryland and North Carolina, both 9–3.

The seven-team Atlantic Coast Conference tournament started Thursday, March 7. The Wolfpack had a first round bye and then, in the semifinals, breezed past Virginia, 87–66, setting up a tournament finale against Maryland. Against the Cavaliers, State was sluggish in the first half, leading 29–27 at intermission. But, in the second half, with Thompson knocking in 37 points for the game, the Wolfpack dominated 58–39.

In the other bracket, Maryland and North Carolina easily dispatched Duke and Wake Forest in the first round; in the semifinals, Maryland advanced to the finals, defeating the Tar Heels 105–85, to set up a third meeting with the Wolfpack and a chance for only one team to get to the NCAA tournament.

There's no doubt in anyone's mind, anyone who has watched ACC basketball since its inception, that the finals of the 1974 ACC tournament was the greatest game ever in the league. It was a tooth and nail battle that went to overtime before State won, 103–100.

David Thompson had a good night, knocking in 10 of 24 field goals and 9 of 11 free throws for 29 points, playing all 43 minutes. But dramatic play by two other Wolfpack players was the key to State's victory.

Tommy Burleson, left off of the All-Atlantic Coast Conference first team, had a career outing, going against Len Elmore and others. Burleson used his sky-hook to convert 18 of 25 field goal shots along with 2 of 4 free throws for a game-high 38 points.

And, Monte Towe had 8 assists and scored 17 points on 7 of 11 field goals and 3 of 4 free throws, 2 of which came with 6 seconds in the overtime when he had cramps in his legs. His last 2 points gave State the final margin of victory.

Each team used only seven players. Maryland shot 61% from the floor. State was at 55%. State had 37 rebounds to Maryland's 31. It was from the free throw line that State had a big advantage with 15 good shots on 26 tries while Maryland was just 6 of 8. The inside game of Burleson and the close defensive coverage of Thompson were key in causing the Terps to foul.

210

Chapter 70

Pack edges out Terps: Amen, amen

Reprinted from the Technician, March 11, 1974

By Jim Pomeranz

Sports Editor

GREENSBORO—The biggest game of the season was to get underway at 8:40 p.m.

The time was 7:45.

Maryland band players were tuning their instruments to "North Carolina," the state's theme song.

The time was 8:00.

"Maryland, My Maryland" could be heard loud and clear throughout the Greensboro Coliseum—played by the Terrapin band, of course.

The time was 8:03.

Retaliation time. State's pep band struck up the NCSU fight song with caissons and all.

The time was 8:10.

State's band had played two good rounds of the Wolfpack fight song, and now it was Maryland's turn again. Not a fight song, but it was loud. Loud enough so everyone would see who was playing.

The time was 8:18.

State returned the favor with another song. Applause filled the arena. The crowd was with the Wolfpack band.

The time was 8:25.

Maryland's basketball team was on the court practicing. State's was in the dressing room.

The time was 8:30.

Here's the Wolfpack. The band struck up five rounds of the caissons again, and the crowd went wild.

The time was 8:39.38.

State's band had played the national anthem, and it was time for one more caisson before the game started. The crowd went wild.

Maryland's band tried to get a few songs into the act, but the yelling for the Wolfpack prevented many people from hearing them.

The time was 8:40.

The ball went up in the air, and State controlled the tap. Maryland, though, burst into the lead and held it the majority of the game. State fans had been subdued except for a few bright moments when the Pack rallied.

The game went on in the second half, tooth and nail. State built a 5-point lead, and Maryland wiped it out. Maryland's band and fans tried to show up the combined efforts of the State, Carolina, Duke, Wake Forest, Clemson, and Virginia cheering sections. "Go Terps Go" could faintly be heard.

The Pack was not to be denied. Tied 97–97 with no time on the clock, overtime began. The crowd began yelling louder and louder. Both bands wanted to play all the time, and they did.

The lead changed hands four times in the extra period. Each time, the fans got on their feet to cheer their favorite team.

There were 6 seconds remaining on the clock in the best basketball game ever.

Monte Towe stepped to the line and sank 2 clutch free throws. The scoreboard showed State in the lead, 103–100.

Maryland could not score.

State had won the 1974 ACC basketball tournament.

The crowd stood and began to cheer:

"Amen, amen, amen."

Chapter 71

Burleson: Pivotman gives first team performance

Reprinted from the Technician, March 11, 1974

By Jim Pomeranz

Sports Editor

Tommy Burleson had been quite a few sports writers' pick for second team All-ACC this season. But funny enough, he was considered good enough to make second team All-American.

Many people began to wonder if the pick for the second ACC team would make the 7'4" center angry sometime in the future. Specifically, would Burleson show the conference writers exactly what he could do with the roundball in the ACC tournament?

The whole story can be summed up with 38 points, 13 rebounds, a few blocked shots, and intimidation.

That's how Tommy Burleson performed against Maryland in State's championship win over the Terrapins, 103–100.

Tommy had been left off the first team all-conference, and the coaches in the conference were hoping Burleson would not be created into a super player because of it.

Virginia coach Bill Gibson was looking forward to playing State in the semi-finals, but he dreaded having to play against Burleson.

"Tommy is upset about not making first team All-ACC, and he will be out to prove something," Gibson declared after his Cavaliers had defeated Clemson, 68–63, Thursday night. "I hope he doesn't."

The next night, as State beat Virginia, 87–66, even though Burleson was not considered the star for the Wolfpack, the big man scored 15 points and pulled down 11 rebounds.

Burleson was devastating against Maryland. One advantage he has over opposing centers is his hook shot. When Tommy spins around and flings the ball towards the rim, it is already on its downward path, and any hand touching the ball is called for goal tending.

Tommy hooked many shots, and was always putting in layups, but what he did with a high degree of greatness was shoot from the outside. Burleson banked shots in from eight and ten feet, continuously.

"I'm happy Tom Burleson had a super game," State head coach Norm Sloan commented after the game.

"Burleson had a fabulous, fabulous night," complimented Maryland head coach Lefty Driesell after the game. "We tried fronting him; we tried siding him. Nothing worked. He was super fired up and leaving him off the first team got him super fired up."

David Thompson, who added 29 points for State against Maryland, got into the Burleson comment column. "Tommy played the greatest game of his career," stated the State All-American. "He was the man tonight."

In the dressing room, Driesell walked up to Burleson, shook his hand and said, "That was the greatest game I've ever seen a big man play. Good luck in the NCAA."

Before the game was over, Burleson had jumped higher than he had in his career and had gone to the basket more than he had in any previous contest. He played a super ball game. He is a super player.

And appropriately, he was awarded the Everett Case Award for being the Most Valuable Player of the tournament. It was the second year in a row he collected the cherished trophy, and it was much deserved.

Chapter 72

The waiting is over

Editorial reprinted from the Technician, March 11, 1974

Pick a hero, any hero in State's overtime victory over Maryland Saturday night in the championship game of the ACC tournament. The thrilling 103–100 Wolfpack win will surely go down in the record books as one of the greatest games ever played throughout the history of the conference.

Monte Towe, Moe Rivers, Phil Spence, Tim Stoddard, and yes, the great David Thompson each carried the Pack's banner at crucial times in the hotly contested triumph. But none carried the banner quite so high (that's right) as 7'4" Tommy Burleson, State's "second string" all-conference center. His performance that night, which incidentally won him the tourney's MVP award for the second consecutive year, will be talked about long after he hangs up his red-and-white jersey for the last time.

However, take nothing away from the Terrapins. Their performance during the ACC tournament set new marks in the record book. Indeed, for their first 90 minutes of playing time in the tournament, the Terps threatened to transform this year's tourney into a showcase of their own talents, blitzing past Duke, Carolina, and, for a while, the Wolfpack. Maryland's domination of the Tar Heels in the semi-final round was certainly unexpected and definitely awesome.

The Maryland team that the Pack met and defeated on two earlier occasions this season was certainly a much improved team in the tournament. Certainly much credit should go to coach Lefty Driesell and his team for their overall showing in the tournament. The Terps were a different team following their loss to the Wolfpack in Cole Field House last month. Should State go on to win the NCAA championship, it is entirely logical to assume that Saturday night's contest was the one that decided the national championship. Even the most devout Pack followers must admit that it is a shame that both teams could not represent the ACC in the NCAA tournament. As this goes to press, neither Maryland nor Carolina have been invited to the NIT, but both are deserving of a bid, and we hope both do go.

As for the Wolfpack, it is certainly poetic justice that it now gets the chance to test its mettle in the NCAA's following its second perfect conference showing on top of last year's 27–0 season. All those theories on what might have been can now be tested for their validity. Thousands of self-appointed "coaches" in this area can now see how their game strategy would work.

All Wolfpack followers have waited eagerly for this moment ever since State capped its perfect season last year with the tournament crown. Now the Pack has the chance, and win or lose, it will certainly be a monumental year for Wolfpack basketball.

Chapter 73

Confident or cocky?

The NCAA tournament was made for the Wolfpack. There were 25 teams invited, 7 in the East region and 6 in each of the West, Mideast, and Midwest regions. The brackets were aligned so that the teams advancing from the East and West would meet in the NCAA Final Four semifinals in Greensboro. State was top seed in the East with a first round bye and into the East semifinals, played in Reynolds Coliseum.

Providence beat Penn to become the Wolfpack's next opponent. Pittsburgh beat St. Joseph's and Furman knocked off South Carolina to set up the other East region semifinals game. And Pitt beat Furman to face the winner of the State-Providence game.

In the West, UCLA and San Francisco drew byes. Dayton beat Cal State Los Angeles to face UCLA; New Mexico beat Idaho State to play San Francisco. The two bye teams advanced, and UCLA beat San Francisco to get to Greensboro.

In the Mideast, Marquette won 3 games to gain a berth in Greensboro, beating Ohio, Vanderbilt, and Michigan. The Wolverines knocked off Notre Dame, which defeated Austin Peay to face Marquette in the Mideast finals.

And in the Midwest, Kansas and Louisville had first round byes. Creighton beat Texas before losing to Kansas, and Oral Roberts defeated Syracuse and then beat Louisville before losing to Kansas.

State's first game in the NCAA tournament was against the eighth-ranked Providence Friars, a team with a 25–3 record led by guard Kevin Stacom and center Marvin Barnes, a consensus All-America. Both were averaging 22 points, and Barnes was pulling down a nation-leading 18 rebounds a game.

Barnes was either very confident or very cocky. "When I get going, there's nothing I can't do on the court, and no one can stop me," he said.

The Wolfpack took the challenge, playing on its home court of Reynolds Coliseum on a Thursday night at 9:00 p.m. Usually, the results of a late Thursday game would never make it into the Friday edition of the Technician, but this time, the game story made it and onto the front page.

Chapter 74

State wins:
Dazzlin' Dave scores 40, leads Pack past Providence

Reprinted from the Technician, March 15, 1974

By Jim Pomeranz

Sports Editor

As one sportswriter put it, "That last basket was worth the price of admission."

Instant Replay:

There were 12 seconds left on the clock. State's Tommy Burleson grabbed the rebound off of Providence backboard. "Tommy," came the yell from guard Monte Towe, half way down the court.

The pass from 7–4 down to 5–5 would have threaded a needle: a swift, straight, but graceful, throw.

Towe pocketed the ball in his hands like a catcher does a baseball, spun his back to the Wolfpack's basket, and flipped the ball backwards high in the air toward the hoop.

And then out of nowhere, there he was: David Thompson. "Alley-oop" they call it. He just scooped the ball out of the air, twisted once, and then laid it in.

That was the last basket.

The final score: 92–78.

And in actuality, the last basket was worth more than the price of admission. The odds makers in Las Vegas had picked the Wolfpack by only 13 points.

State now advances to the championship of the Eastern Regional and will play Pittsburgh at 12:10 p.m. Saturday. The Panthers downed the Furman Paladins, 81–78.

The whole game seemed like "alley-oop" as All-American David Thompson scored 40 points to lead the Pack to victory, with most of his scoring developing from the lob high above the basket.

"David had a fantastic night," applauded State coach Norm Sloan. "And he capped it off with Monte (Towe) with a real showman's act at the end."

"I don't know how to play that play," observed defeated Friar coach Dave Gavitt about the "alley-oop." "He's (Thompson) so exceptional."

Thompson's superb performance combined with Burleson's 16 points and a career high 24 rebounds, Towe's 15 points and evasive ball handling, Morris Rivers' 11 points, and super defense by Phil Spence and Tim Stoddard gave State the edge throughout the night.

Spence and Stoddard held Providence All-American Marvin Barnes to only 14 points.

Chapter 75

He tripped over Spence's shoulder

And then came the fall.

It was in the finals of the Eastern Regional. State was playing Pittsburgh:

A game the Wolfpack would win easily 100–72;

A game in which David Thompson would play only 10 minutes and score just 8 points;

A game in which the Wolfpack only led by 47–41 at the half but turned it on in the second period not only to take the regional title and a shot at UCLA in the national semifinals but to win one for Thompson who leaped so high trying to block a shot that he tripped over Phil Spence's shoulder, landing on his head, knocking him out, and sending him to the hospital. It created an eerily quiet throughout Reynolds Coliseum mid-Saturday afternoon, stopping play for what seemed like forever.

In the lead story of Monday, March 18, headlined "Thompson's fall not serious," this is how the paper summed it up in a non-bylined story:

> Wolfpack basketball star David Thompson was released from
> Rex Hospital late Sunday morning following a night of routine

observation after his head-over-heels fall in Saturday's Eastern Regional championship game with Pittsburgh.

Thompson suffered a gash on the back of his head after tumbling over Phil Spence in an attempt to block a shot. He came down on the back of his head and neck, rendering him unconscious for four minutes. He was taken to the hospital for examination and returned to the State bench late in the game and watched as the Wolfpack blitzed Pittsburgh 100–72 and helped cut down the nets following the game. He stayed long enough to don his street clothes and return to the hospital to spend the night.

A hospital spokesman termed Thompson's condition as "satisfactory" and anticipated no "delayed aftereffects" from his concussion, which resulted in 15 stitches. His is expected to resume practice this week and should start against UCLA this Saturday in the NCAA finals at Greensboro.

When Thompson returned to the coliseum following his accident, he was given a standing ovation by the sellout crowd and was embraced by several teammates who came off the court to greet him.

In his Sunday basketball show, coach Norm Sloan said, "I thought the near tragedy of what happened yesterday was the greatest display of love and affection for a group of people, for one individual, and concern for an individual I have ever seen in my life. I know that the ball game and the season became totally meaningless to us and the members of the squad when David had his accident."

Sloan added that Thompson had an "excellent night" at Rex Hospital.

The coach also noted that CBS news director Walter Cronkite called yesterday to inquire about the All-American's condition.

"He was watching the show in New York and tracked down as to where David was going to be taken and had a phone call waiting there and talked to one of the physicians personally about his condition by the time he arrived," Sloan said.

In the game, Tommy Burleson led all scorers with 26 points. Monte Towe's 19 points matched the high scorer from Pitt. Morris Rivers had 17 points.

After the game, the players voiced their concern for Thompson; *Technician* editorial writers criticized the game officials, and UCLA coach John Wooden started a "mind game" as his Bruins and the Wolfpack were headed for a rematch of the December showdown between the nation's top two teams.

Chapter 76

Thompson:

State players were concerned for All-American

Reprinted from the Technician, March 18, 1974

By Bill Moss

Staff Writer

The future of State basketball was plunged into darkness Saturday afternoon when David Thompson hit the floor with a horrifying thud.

The 53 wins out of the Wolfpack's last 54 games, the ACC championship, the Eastern Regional, somehow, with David lying still on that basketball floor, all these things became meaningless.

They carried him away to the hospital, and the game continued, but the shadow still lingered inside the coliseum. Not until David sent word that he was okay did the light appear once again.

State, inspired to win the game for their fallen teammate, went on to rout Pittsburgh, 100–72 for the championship of the Eastern Regional.

For the players, however, deep concern for David made the victory seem secondary. There was no jubilation in the locker room on this day, only relief and thankfulness that Thompson was okay.

Listening to Monte Towe, it was apparent that the accident had shaken him. "I thought David had broken his neck," he said. "After he got hurt, I just went through the motions. Now I just hope he's going to be alright. I'm concerned about him as a person, not as a player."

Tommy Burleson, who tied with Thompson in the voting for the (regional) most valuable player, pointed to the team play after the injury.

"We were emotional when David went out, and we seemed to play together more. No one individual felt he had to pick up the slack. It was just everybody coming together."

Phil Spence sat in the locker room and talked about Thompson's fall. The concern could still be seen on his face as he recalled what happened.

"I was trying to block for the rebound," he said. "He went over my back. When I saw what happened, man I was scared."

When David regained consciousness, his immediate concern was for the game.

Each player knew his job was to work that much harder to make up for the loss of the All-American forward. Morris Rivers played an excellent game, hitting on 8 of 12 attempts from the floor, grabbing 8 rebounds, and handing out 3 assists.

But this was no one-man show. Towe played hard, and as he fought back tears, he directed the offense. Spence came in and pulled down 14 rebounds, passed deftly for 4 assists, and finished with 10 points. It was a team win for the Wolfpack on Saturday. They proved they can win without Thompson, but still, everyone would have been much happier if he had been in there. Phil Spence said, "With him, we're much better. Without him, we're still a good team."

Chapter 77

Keep ACC out of barroom brawls

Editorial reprinted from the Technician, March 18, 1974

The Eastern Regional tournament this year was marred by two events: the tragic injury to David Thompson and the extremely poor performance by the referees throughout the tournament.

Certainly one of the most frightening moments in State's athletic history was the sight of Thompson sprawled unconscious on the court after his leaping attempt to block a shot, falling over teammate Phil Spence in the process, and landing on the back of his head. It is extremely fortunate that the young All-American suffered nothing more than lacerations on the back of his head. During the time it took to revive Thompson, which seemed like an eternity, all State fans at the game and watching on television feared the worst.

Emotionally charged, the Wolfpack went on to rout Pittsburgh and gain a berth in the NCAA semi-finals in Greensboro, proving that the Wolfpack was certainly more than a one-man show. During the closing minutes of the first half, State actually had four non-starters in the game, and when Tommy Burleson picked up his fourth foul early in the second half, coach Norm Sloan countered with three substitutes in the front line, an unusual move even for a team as deep as the

Wolfpack. Sloan's charges certainly showed they had character Saturday.

Now consider this. Had the officiating been any better in the tournament, and there was considerable room for improvement, Thompson's injury might have never occurred. On his previous trip down court, Thompson thought he was fouled while shooting and hesitated before returning to the other end. We all know what happened next.

There has been considerable talk about the officiating in the regional, and well there should have been. Most notable was the State-Providence game Thursday night, which at times resembled a football contest. The officiating during the entire event was of very low quality. Although it has become customary for ACC fans to second-guess referees during regular season games, it would be safe to say that any fan would prefer the conference's own referees instead of the ones brought in for the regional.

To insure "equality" in the respective regional tournaments, the NCAA assigns referees from different conferences to officiate the games. The referees assigned to the Eastern Regionals were supposed to be the best from the Big 8, the Missouri Valley, and the Southwest conferences. If it pleases the NCAA, we in the ACC would just as soon not participate in the barroom brawls that these other conferences must have.

If Thompson was confused by the inconsistent officiating, he had ample justification to be. Later in the Pittsburgh contest, Moe Rivers also went down, making many spectators wonder if they were not actually witnesses to a mass mugging. However, the inspired play of the entire team overcame the deficiencies in the officiating. The display of emotion by the team and by the entire coliseum when Thompson returned from Rex Hospital shows what respect the Shelby native has earned during his career here. Although many observers considered the

ACC championship game with Maryland the best they've ever seen, certainly something has to be said for this game as well. Because it was in this game that the Wolfpack stopped being a great team and instead became a legend.

Chapter 78

UCLA's Wooden points to December

Reprinted from the Technician, March 18, 1974

State's Norm Sloan is not about to "get involved in any media psychological warfare" over the Wolfpack's Saturday rematch with UCLA.

The Bruin's John Wooden already has.

"I just want them to remember the December game and then ask themselves if they are entitled to a psychological edge," commented Wooden after UCLA had defeated San Francisco, 83–60, in the NCAA Western Regional championship. That win, coupled with the Wolfpack's win over Pitt Saturday, sets up a battle between the nation's first and second rated college basketball teams.

Wooden said he hoped the Wolfpack would dwell on the fact that the Bruins beat State by 18 points on a neutral court earlier. The game Saturday will be played in the Greensboro Coliseum before what could be a highly partisan Wolfpack crowd.

Sunday, Sloan reviewed the first contest between the two schools.

"What I remember about it is first, we lost by 18 points," he said, "and number two, Bill Walton, who is so important to their basketball team, didn't play but about half the basketball game. Of course, a whole season has transpired since we first played. Both teams are different now than they were then"

Sloan said he did not want State's team to view the upcoming game as one for revenge.

"I want them to think about playing our basketball game defensively and offensively and getting on the boards and so forth," he commented. "We would be making a terrible mistake if we went into this thing looking at it as a revenge situation.

"It's a basketball game for the national championship," he continued. "It's the semifinals of the finals, and that's the way I want us to look at it. We've worked hard and played hard. We have a great basketball team and a wonderful bunch of guys. They have as much going for them as far as ability, as far as attitude, closeness, love, and appreciation for one another as any group I have ever known.

"This is what I want us to remember and concentrate on," Sloan stated. "I don't want us to spend a lot of time thinking about UCLA wanting us to think about them. I've said all along that the UCLA game was the thirteenth most important game on our schedule. Now it is the most important. That's the only thing that has changed."

Chapter 79

100 tickets to ride

There were 100 tickets available for students for the NCAA games in Greensboro at $20, which covered all games. Because of demand, students had to sign up on Monday and Tuesday that week for a drawing for the tickets. There were 2,734 students who entered the lottery. The drawing was held Tuesday evening, and the winners were announced in Wednesday's *Technician*.

The lucky 100 included Clinton Barry Albright, Marilyn Allen, Bob Anton, Janet Lynn Bahor, Thomas B. Baird, Marian S. Beightol, Robert Thomas Benton, William Bradham, Forrest E. Brown, Ward Ross Burtnette,

David M. Butler, George Clark, Gregg Cody, Joseph R. Conard, Pat Connolly, Susan Cooper, John Lewis Cottrell, Jr., Curtis Davis, Phillip K. Davis, Charles Thomas Edgerton,

Robert Glenn Eure, Rocky Faircloth, Christopher X. Fedor, John Ferebee, Bonnie G. Fleming, Neil Fleming, Preston Gaster, Robert L. Geren, Charles D. Greene, Peaches Gunter,

Robert E. Hamlin, Michael Kevin Hanes, John Harper, Gerald Hartmann, Greg Hawkins, Steve Hendricks, Charles Highsmith, William Andrew Hobbs, James H. Holcombe, Wayne A Howell,

Clyde Neal Humphrey, Tony Leary, Myra Gaye Lentz, Bruce Lingerfelt, Michael C. Lockamy, T. A. Lovin, Lynn Mcclelland, Richard F. May, Steve Moneypenny, William Reece Morgan, Rusty Morris,

Terry Wayne Nance, Victoria Newell, Jack D. Norman, John Obermiller, Harvey Odom, Davie Oettinger, David Oliver, J. L. Outlaw, Charles Patnode, Alec Perry,

D. Ladd Perry, Lawrence Petrouick, James E. Phillips, Forrest E. Putnam, James Reeves, Richard L. Robertson, Jonathan Alan Rosselet, Sam Sarvis, Mrs. Odell Shambley, Ken Sheesley,

Robert C. Siewers, Randy Simmons, Lawrence Michael Smith, Ronald Snider, Eddie Spach, Jerry W. Strickland, Glendel L. Tucker, Doug Von Valkenburgh, Rick Walker, Timothy L. West,

Jimmy Williams, Leon F. Williams III, Joe L. Williams, W. Michael Williams, Donald E. Winchell, John William Woodard, Glenn Woolard, Rick A. Wooteen, Allen R. Wooten, and Richard Worley.

Those were the lucky 100 with tickets to ride, to gain admission to Greensboro, to see the Wolfpack in its rematch with UCLA. All wanted to be there for David Thompson's return to action. As the week progressed, so did Thompson.

Chapter 80

Thompson regains form in practice

Reprinted from the Technician, March 20, 1974

By Jim Pomeranz

Sports Editor

Basketball practice started at the usual time Tuesday afternoon for the number one nationally ranked Wolfpack but under many different circumstances.

First, State began getting ready for a rematch with the UCLA Bruins.

Second, the Wolfpack is not only headed for a collision with UCLA, but the national finals happen to be the reason for the Saturday rematch, and State is out to win that.

Thirdly, over 1,000 fans sat in the stands watching as practice got underway. But they were there because of the fourth circumstance.

David Thompson was back with the Pack, but back with the Pack only after a speedy recovery after a very bad fall in State's 100–72 victory over Pitt in the finals of the Eastern Regional.

He started off his workout at a slow pace, not jumping as high as usual but with behind the back passes still there, however, at first, not as swift as before.

Then the workout became swifter. DT jumped a little higher, ran a little faster, and shot a little sharper.

The other players began using the dunk shot on their layups. The crowd edged toward the front of their seats in hopes the All-American from Shelby would add a little razzle-dazzle with the stuff shot.

He practiced with a small bandage on the back of his head and still seemed a little wary of his moves. But then with a little bit of coaxing from his teammates...whoosh!

He dunked it.

Softly at first, as if to make sure of himself, but soon he was raring to go.

Applause and yells came from the crowd after each joyous shot.

Fans continued to watch in excitement as the whole team got in the swing of things.

An alley-oop pass came from Thompson to Tommy Burleson. Swoosh! Dunk again.

Spence, Moeller, Nuce, Hawkins—they all jumped high into the air and slammed the ball through the hoop. All, but one.

Monte Towe didn't seem left out. He can't quite get up that high, but how many 5'7" basketball players can?

But he still received requests from the crowd for the exciting shot.

Once in a three-on-two situation, Towe had the ball well down the middle of the lane. He jumped up and challenged Burleson. Out of one section of fans, a high voice, that of a small girl admirer, cried, "Dunk it, Monte."

Thompson was still regaining his superb form. He was in the middle of a crowd under the basket when a Spence shot hit the front of the rim and bounced high into the air.

Up, up, and away DT flew, grabbing the ball and throwing it through the center of the hoop.

David Thompson definitely returned to practice Tuesday afternoon and showed great form. Great enough to let the world know he's back for the Pack.

Chapter 81

Wolfpack winds up home practice before 5,000 fans

Reprinted from the Technician, March 22, 1974

By Jim Pomeranz

Sports Editor

The number one nationally ranked Wolfpack basketball team completed home practices Thursday prior to the NCAA finals and the Saturday rematch with UCLA.

And as other practices for the past week, it was no ordinary workout.

Approximately 5,000 fans poured into the Reynolds Coliseum to get a glimpse of the practice. Little kids lined the courtside and yelled kind remarks to their favorite players. State students sat in their seats and cheered the team through the semi-scrimmage. And the older fans smiled and applauded as the squad turned a light workout into a Broadway show.

It was like follow the leader, at times.

The team clapped their hands. The crowd clapped their hands.

The show continued.

"Dunk it David!" cried a young admirer.

And he did, with show and all.

The graceful player dribbled toward the basket, leaped into the air, swung the ball around his waist, glided past the basket, and then

237

guided the ball in front of his face to behind his head and through the nets—swoosh!

Then it was Tom Burleson's turn.

The 7'4" frame player caught a pass on his way to the basket and dribbled toward the hoop. But after he had passed by the basket, unlike Thompson who had to leap up a couple of feet, Burleson barely left the floor as he slammed the ball through the cylinder and onto the floor—dunk, again.

But the little kids still wanted Monte Towe to perform the magical trick.

Laughing, he grabbed the ball, went up toward the basket as high as he could, extended his arms behind his head, and flung the ball at the hoop. But his toss was in an upward direction. Towe just doesn't have that high leap.

The practice session lasted only 30 minutes but couldn't have ended any better.

The Wolfpack was in its usual three on two fast break drill when head coach Norm Sloan walked onto the court to end practice.

Thompson was bringing the ball down court and, instead of stopping, began approaching the half court mark. Sloan was still motioning to stop.

As Thompson saw him, he leaped into the air and released the ball some 30 feet away.

That shot was as graceful as any shot the All-American has ever attempted. The ball raced to the goal. If there had been a dime on the edge of the hoop, it would probably still be there now. As the ball finished its arcing process and entered the cylinder of the hoop, it was evident it would not touch a bit of metal.

The swish shot barely touched the nets and only for a fraction of a second.

The crowd rose to its feet and gave the Wolfpack a thunderous roar of approval.

"Let's go to Greensboro," came shouts from one end of the Coliseum. "Let's go to Greensboro. We're ready."

Chapter 82

Wolfpack overcomes Bruins, 80–77

Reprinted from the Technician, March 25, 1974

By Jim Pomeranz

Sports Editor

GREENSBORO—They never said die.

The tension, the excitement, the enthusiasm, the competitiveness were all present. Two basketball teams full of talent, ranked number one and number two in the nation, having met once before in the history of the schools were scheduled to battle for the second time.

ST. LOUIS (Dec.15)—Top ranked UCLA, led by a come-off-the-bench performance by All-American Bill Walton in the last 10 minutes of action, defeated second ranked North Carolina State, 84–66.

The season continued with State winning every game they played, and UCLA dominating every game they played until Notre Dame, Oregon, and Oregon State. The Bruins had three losses headed into NCAA playoffs and three overtimes in the West Regional before they won. The Bruins struggled but still won.

After the loss to the Irish, quotes such as "This assures them (UCLA) of the national title" and "They'll never be defeated again this season" were heard across the nation.

They never said die.

State marched along, sweeping the ACC regular season without a loss, and then winning a great battle with Maryland in the finals of the ACC tournament.

The big game was set all over again.

Here, in the Greensboro Coliseum on Saturday, March 23, on national television, the number one and number two teams were to meet for the second time in the same season.

But the roles were reversed. State, top ranked, and UCLA, in the second slot, were headed into a showdown game, and all the world would be waiting to hear the results.

But hold it a minute. In St. Louis, the top team was favored. And in this game, UCLA was again picked to win, by 5½ points to be exact.

Kansas and Marquette were on the court playing around, with the Warriors on top. But were the fans interested? Well, considering that most of the 15,829 people in attendance were Wolfpack fans, no!

"I wish this game would get over with so the real action could start," stated red-coated observers.

The Warriors finished off the Jayhawks and then returned to see who they would play in the championship contest.

Big Bill Walton and tall Tom Burleson met in center circle for the opening tap. The action started, and the game was finally here.

The red-headed All-American hit the first two points of the game. The Bruin fans went wild, all 800.

The Wolfpack dominated the first half and built a 5-point lead. But UCLA came back, and on a 30-foot shot by Dave Myers with one second on the clock in the first period, the score was tied 35–35.

Start a new game.

UCLA burst out to an 11-point lead early in the second half.

They never said die.

The Wolfpack fought back, and they had the victory. The score was once again tied, 65–65, with 48 seconds remaining in the game, and State went for one shot. But it was short, and overtime was declared.

Only 2 points were scored by each team in the next 5 minutes. The crowd went wild as "there will be a second 5-minute overtime" was announced over the PA system.

The Bruins came out sparking, and before any State fan could bat an eye, 7 points were added to UCLA's score. Things got quiet around the coliseum

But, they never said die.

"Time out, State."

"He (State head coach Norm Sloan) told us to press them all over the floor and make turnovers," explained Tim Stoddard. "That's all we could do."

The Pack reappeared onto the court to a thunderous roar of approval and immediately outscored the Bruins 13–3 in the remaining 3½ minutes.

The top team in the nation, the State Wolfpack, never said die, and they won, 80–77.

Chapter 83

Warriors win: Marquette challenges Pack in finale

Reprinted from the Technician, March 25, 1974

By Jim Pomeranz

Sports Editor

GREENSBORO—After defeating mighty UCLA, 80–77, State's Wolfpack faces Marquette tonight for the 1974 NCAA championship. The Warriors defeated the Kansas Jayhawks, 64–51, in semi-final action to gain the final berth.

Junior center Maurice Lucas led Marquette with 18 points. Marcus Washington added 16 for the Warriors.

"I'm sort of proud of myself for picking Marquette in that Mideast regional," stated State head coach Norm Sloan after the Pack defeated UCLA 80–77. "I've been very impressed with them this year.

"They have some fine players," he continued, "and they are in a very enviable position."

Besides Lucas and Washington, Marquette starts 6–9 freshman Maurice Ellis, sophomore Earl Tatum, and 6' pointman Lloyd Walton.

"Our only problem will be getting down to earth," warned Sloan. "But we have overcome too many things not to come back down for that game."

Marquette's win over Kansas started out slow and close with Kansas leading at the half, 24–23. Neither team could manage over 40% field goal shooting in the first period.

But in the second half, the Warriors came out fired up and jumped to a lead that was never relinquished.

The championship game between the Pack and the Warriors will get underway at 9:10 p.m. and can be seen on the NBC television network. UCLA and Kansas will battle at 7:00 p.m. for third place.

Chapter 84

Covering SPORTS: Tickets and big wig fat cats

Reprinted from the Technician, March 25, 1974

By Jim Pomeranz

Sports Editor

GREENSBORO—The official attendance for the semi-final games in the NCAA tournament was announced as 15,829. That is the largest crowd to see a basketball game in the Greensboro Coliseum, and considering that only 4,000 tickets were divided among the four competing schools, that's pretty good attendance.

The tickets that were sent to the four schools were divided in various ways.

Tickets at State were divided into three categories. Students received 100, the Wolfpack Club was awarded 700 tickets, and 200 tickets went to players' parents, the administration, and other similar and related groups.

At Marquette, the story was different. Students there were lucky enough to get 300 of the 1,000 available precious slips of paper, and the 700 remaining ducats went to alumni and administration.

The situation at Kansas was similar to the Marquette distribution,

And at UCLA, the students could have as many as they wanted. A sports writer from the *Daily Bruin* sitting next to me at the game explained that their athletic department told students that if the students wanted tickets, they would be able to get all they needed. Of course, knowing that not too many students can afford the trip from Los Angeles to Greensboro, a statement like that is expected. But the fact is that the students from UCLA had the opportunity to buy many more than the students at State.

A week ago at the Eastern Regional at Reynolds Coliseum, Bruin assistant coach Frank Arnold was having a problem scouting the Furman-Pitt game because the Furman cheerleaders were sitting on the floor in front of him and would continuously jump up and yell. Of course, he could rarely see the floor.

In a talk about the fan situation with State assistant athletic director Frank Weedon, Arnold expressed his belief that the game was "for the kids," but he would like a seat with a clearer view for scouting purposes. He later explained he meant that all college sports were for the students at the schools first and for other people second.

Weedon did not come right out and acknowledge that statement, but his nodding head confirmed what Arnold had said.

Now, we understand the argument the athletic department gives about money contributions through the Wolfpack Club being needed to pay for the success of programs such as basketball and football, but athletics at colleges and universities started for the students, so why change now?

Students contribute about $215,000 each year in mandatory fees to the athletic department and no telling how much through the Student Supply Store.

The Wolfpack Club gives about $600,000 each year, most of which goes to scholarships.

Students deserve more tickets to such events as the NCAA finals, the Big Four tournament, and the ACC tournament. But we do not get them. And it is because of the 6,000 Wolfpack Club members, those big wig fat cats that have worked their butts off in a business so they don't have to suffer any more.

But what do they do when they come to a game? Most of the time, the men in the red coats view the game while stuck on their posteriors, and they yell at the refs.

The students are the ones that yell for the team. They are the ones that give the players that boost when needed. It happened at the State victory over UCLA here Saturday. When the team got down, it was the students that started the yelling. Later, the Wolfpack Club joined in.

There are 14,000 students at State, and next year, enrollment is expected to increase to 15,000. But will the number of seats for these extra events increase for the students?

If the students don't make a fuss over the ticket situation, the most vocal and most supporting Wolfpack group will never get any more tickets than they do now.

Tickets allotted the school for any extra athletic events should be allotted to the students and the Wolfpack Club members using a formula that includes both the amount of money each group contributes and the number of members in each group.

Chapter 85

A 'students vs. police' thing?

The win over UCLA kicked off a wild celebration in Raleigh, one that started about late Saturday afternoon and lasted late into the night until 1 a.m. Sunday when police in riot gear arrived, creating an ugly scene that somewhat dampened the celebration.

Howard Barnett, news editor for the *Technician*, pieced together a Monday, March 25, front page story based on eyewitness accounts and interviews with police, members of the university administration, and individuals. Here is part of his report:

> Riot geared Raleigh police moved onto Hillsborough Street late Saturday night to clear celebrating crowds in the aftermath of State's victory over UCLA earlier during the day.
>
> Victory demonstrations started at about 5:30 p.m., were interrupted briefly by rain, and concluded with tear gas, night sticks, beer bottles, and bruises early Sunday morning.
>
> At about 9:00, the Raleigh police arrived at Hillsborough Street and Oberlin Road, where a large crowd had gathered. They ordered the people to disperse, after which they attempted to clear the vicinity with tear gas. The police, wearing helmets and wielding night sticks, cleared Hillsborough Street from Oberlin Road to Pullen Road.

Chancellor Caldwell came out to the area from his home, which fronts the besieged block, to urge the students to move the rally to the brickyard but received little support.

"I then tried to get the students to disperse," Caldwell said, "but nobody would. After a while, I decided I wasn't serving any purpose, so I went inside for a while, just listening to what was being said."

Several students were arrested, including one for streaking, and others for "disorderly conduct and use of obscene language." After this initial confrontation, the police left the area.

The demonstration continued unchecked until about 11:45 when two other police cars arrived, apparently to investigate a small accident near the crowd. They were greeted with yells and beat a hasty retreat, followed by several beer bottles, one of which broke out a tail light. The crowd followed behind the two cars, which headed down Hillsborough Street towards the capitol.

The crowd remained until about 1:00 a.m., when more police arrived with riot equipment and began to clear the street. After using tear gas, they arrested a number of students in an attempt to finally clear the street of people.

The story continued through the eyes of students in the middle of the celebration, some who said they were falsely accused, some who were trying to get home, walking through the area, and some who blamed the ugly part of it on the police for simply showing up. The police reported officers being injured and police cars being damaged.

Robert McPhail, who witnessed the first part of the confrontation, said, "I thought things were going fine until the police came in. The students were about to break up before the police got there. Personally, my whole attitude changed when I saw them beating that guy. I was furious. It became a students versus police thing then."

After the police came for the second time, things became more destructive. A road sign was stolen. As people charged down Hillsborough Street after the two police cars, a rocking chair was stolen from a porch and broken up. About 30 students converged on a moving van that came into the area and rocked it for several minutes. As it moved on, something standing on top of it swung the traffic signals back and forth, turning one around sideways.

"The police instigated it by going there in the first place," said McPhail. "They had no business there."

"Of course, you get only partial views of this thing from people who were there," said Caldwell. "The person standing at one end of the block couldn't see what happened at the other end."

The *Technician* editorial writers also addressed the incident:

...How much the win meant to the student body at State and to the Raleigh public in general was made manifest in the extensive and prolonged celebrations touched off by the game. ... The impetuousness of college youth mixed with the euphoria of the team's giddying accomplishment to produce a tide of mass emotion unseen in this city since the aftermath of Martin Luther King's assassination in 1968. ... The outcome of Saturday's game was cause for great celebration. ... There came a point on Saturday night, however, when the throng on Hillsborough Street ceased to be a group of students enjoying one of the high points of their collegiate careers and became instead an ugly mob, which resisted legitimate efforts on the part of law enforcement officials to disperse. ... The presence of city police in full riot gear surely did little to quell the restlessness of the crowd ... Whatever might have happened, we are still left with the reality of what did occur. Driven by some unknown urge to remain in the street all night and keep the party going, a few hundred youths, perhaps not all of them State students, managed to blight what was an otherwise unforgettable day for followers of the Red and White. ... The number one basketball team in the nation deserves better.

The number one basketball team in the nation, away from the trials and tribulations happening in Raleigh, was holed up in Greensboro and had one more game to play to claim the national title. It was Monday night, March 25, in the Greensboro Coliseum against Marquette.

Chapter 86

Marquette falls; Wolfpack reigns over all the land

Reprinted from the Technician, March 27, 1974

By Jim Pomeranz

Sports Editor

GREENSBORO—It was a great ending to a great season. Maybe the defeating of UCLA seemed to be a bigger accomplishment to many observers, but to the State Wolfpack basketball team, winning the national crown in 1974 was the greatest.

The number one nationally ranked and number one in the NCAA playoffs State Wolfpack defeated Marquette Monday night in Greensboro, 76–64—and what a win!

"It's just a great feeling," explained Tim Stoddard.

"The UCLA win was a great win," stated David Thompson, "but the finals is where we wanted to be."

Monte Towe said the win had not hit him with as much excitement as maybe other games had, but "tomorrow, I'll probably go crazy."

Tom Burleson, who played his last basketball game in a State uniform or as a college player, for that matter, just reflected on his stay with the Wolfpack.

"It's been a lovely four years at NC State," he said. "It's hard to believe it's over."

Burleson, Towe, and Thompson, along with Marquette's Maurice Lucas and UCLA's Bill Walton, were voted to the all-tournament team for their fabulous two days of play in Greensboro. Thompson was named the tournament's most valuable player.

"They're number one," commented Marquette coach Al McGuire about State. "They are a great, great ball club. They were dynamite tonight."

Even though Thompson received MVP honors, many observers thought the key to the Wolfpack victory was Towe, and McGuire agreed.

And toward the end of the game, McGuire even stepped onto the court and gave Towe a handshake of congratulation.

"You can talk about Thompson and Burleson all you want," he said, "but that little white kid in the backcourt is the man. I've got quick kids (on Marquette), but he blew right by them like he was running in the 100-yard dash in the Olympics.

"They got us," he continued. "They're a better ball club."

Towe sparked the Wolfpack with his shots not only from downtown Greensboro, but also from down under the basket. The 5'7" guard tossed in 16 points against the Warriors.

David Thompson complimented the play of the diminutive guard.

"He's definitely a big help," said the All-American. "If you're open, he'll get you the ball." Towe and Thompson have combined throughout the year for some of the most exciting alley-oops plays seen.

"If you give it to him (Towe), he'll bring it up court," continued Thompson. "There's really nothing to worry about."

Thompson even stated, jokingly of course, that the toughest player he ever played against was "Monte in practice."

"This is something every kid dreams about," said Towe after the game. "We've worked awfully hard this year. It feels great right now."

Chapter 87

Go Pack! Loyal fans help State have last say

Reprinted from the Technician, March 27, 1974

GREENSBORO—Much more could not have been asked of the student cheering sections in the 1974 NCAA championship game Monday night. Actually, the enthusiasm shouted throughout the Greensboro Coliseum by the Marquette and State student cheerers began with 7:50 remaining in the UCLA 78–61 consolation victory over Kansas.

"We are Marquette! We are Marquette! We are Marquette!" began the 300 Warriors.

And then after a few minutes of silence, the State pep band stood up, faced the Marquette students, and quietly pronounced in a soft Southern drawl, "We-e-e i-is Sta-a-ate, ya-a-a'll! We-e-e i-is Sta-a-ate, ya-a-a'll!"

That sort of angered the Warrior fans, and with much louder volume, the Marquette students emphatically stated, "We are Marquette! We are Marquette!"

But, of course, that did not stop Wolfpackers all around the coliseum from replying.

"Who are Marquette? Who are Marquette?" questioned the State supporters.

With hands waving toward the State students as if to cast a jinx on them, the Marquette students had to have the last say.

"Go State go; go off the court! Go State go; go off the court."

That's not very original, but "who is Marquette," anyway?

And later in the game, even though Marquette's loss was evident, the Warriors started again.

"We are Marquette!"

But the State students answered, "We are number one! We are number one!"

And, of course, the Wolfpack had the last say, 76–64.

Chapter 88

Greg Lee: "State has only three players: Thompson, Burleson, and Towe"

Reprinted from the Technician, March 29, 1974

By Ray Deltz

Staff Writer

Upon leaving the Greensboro Coliseum Monday night following the Wolfpack's victory over Marquette, this reporter and a travelling companion decided to check in to a local drinking house to reminisce a few to Monte Towe's 30-foot swish shots.

Unfortunately, neither of us was very familiar with the great Greensboro area. So, after we had driven past several pizza houses only to find them closed, a decision was made to really celebrate by feasting at the Waffle House.

After being seated only about 10 minutes, an athletic-looking individual sat down on a nearby stool. His order went something like "three ham omelets, two scrambled eggs, three charburgers..."

It turned out to be UCLA point guard Greg Lee.

Of course, a conversation soon developed.

"What did you think of the two games?" questioned Lee, after seeing the red clothing the two of us were wearing.

"I think both teams could have played better," came the reply.

"If we would have put it together, we would have easily beaten State," quipped Lee. "State has depth, but we have a lot more quality depth than them."

What Lee must not have realized was that only five players may play at one time from each team in the sport of basketball.

"State has only three players: Thompson, Burleson, and Towe," stated the UCLA senior. "Burleson is able to hold his own. Towe is pretty tough, and Thompson is phenomenal.

"But I don't see a lot in Morris Rivers," he continued. "I don't really think its basketball watching Towe all over the floor on his hands and knees. I feel the same way about Stoddard always throwing those elbows."

Lee and teammate Bill Walton have been known to meditate sitting back-to-back before Bruin games. Lee expounded on Walton's reactions to the State win over UCLA.

"I just left Bill a minute ago," he explained. "Oh, he felt Burleson should have fouled out during the first 10 minutes of the game. He thought the referees didn't do a very good job.

"I think it's the same way in the pros," stated the history major from Reseda, California. "The (Milwaukee) Bucks would win it every year if the referees did a consistent job,"

And then there was the question about the weather, considering the snow on Monday morning.

"It's pretty cold," he said. "I'll be anxious to get back to the warm weather in Los Angeles."

That seems like a logical excuse for the Bruins loss: the cold temperature. But then there's next year in San Diego when the Pack will go for the second NCAA title in a row.

Chapter 89

Thousands of students rally on Hillsborough

Reprinted from the Technician, March 27, 1974

By Howard Barnett

News Editor

In a rally much different from the atmosphere of confrontation Saturday, thousands of Wolfpack fans flooded Hillsborough Street Monday night after State clinched the national basketball championship.

While a crowd estimated at 6,000 gathered at the State Capitol building, other fans remained around the entrance to Pullen Road, cheering and tossing rolls of toilet paper into the air.

Police blocked off Hillsborough Street at Woodburn Road and routed traffic around the celebrants but made no move to interfere with the festivities. There were many fireworks in evidence including firecrackers, M-80s, Roman candles, and a few star shells, which burst to the oohs and ahs of the crowd.

Cars that managed to get through the police blockade were drummed on, walked over, and occasionally rocked by the onlookers, but the mood seemed to be generally good-natured.

A mock war developed between the people on top of the Hillsborough Square Restaurant and the people in the street. The air was soon full of chunks of soft, frozen snow, left over from Monday's early morning storm. The defenders on the roof made a barricade of tables but were eventually routed in spite of their efforts.

As time passed, the crowd grew with more displays of fireworks. People in cars honked horns and held up banners proclaiming the Pack's position in the nation: "#1."

At 12:30 a.m., the group that had marched to the capitol got back, filling the block between Pullen Road and Oberlin Road with a solid mass of humanity.

About 5,000 people packed the small area, and after some minutes of yelling and ice-throwing, different contingents began removing road signs from the general vicinity. First to go were two signs saying, "Business-1." These were waived about enthusiastically by their captors and were followed quickly by a street sign and a "Dead End" sign.

One gentleman perched himself on the sign pointing out Andrew Johnson's birthplace. His friends promptly began shaking it back and forth until finally sign, rider, and all came crashing to the ground. He was unhurt, however, and the group spent the next few minutes trying to put the sign back where it came from.

For all the pushing and fireworks in the gathering, there was apparently only one real injury. One girl who said her foot had been run over by a car was taken to a hospital by ambulance. Shortly after that, at about 1:30, the rally broke up.

Chapter 90

Sour note

Editorial reprinted from the Technician, March 27, 1974

Monday night's celebration following State's win over Marquette for the NCAA championship went rather smoothly in relation to Saturday's hoopla. In Saturday's riotous celebration, 31 people were arrested, 9 of them State students. Several injuries were also reported by both police and students. For every police report of vandalism and property damage, students cited numerous incidents when bystanders were roughed up by police with Billy clubs and Mace. Both sides overreacted, and the final result was to be expected.

Monday night, however, instead of confronting students and other participants with riot gear, the police cordoned off the area surrounding the campus. By rerouting traffic away from the campus area and staying clear of the celebration, the police avoided another nasty situation. If this strategy had been put in effect Saturday night, the arrests and injuries might never have happened.

Still, student conduct was not at its best either. Numerous complaints came in to police Saturday night and probably more came in Monday night as well. The area around the campus following the celebration resembled a battlefield. As a matter of fact, several of the students behaved as if a battle was being carried out Monday night.

During the course of the festivities, highway signs were uprooted, and cars were trampled on. Still, more injuries occurred. Property damage was evident following the celebration. The students raised hell at the expense of others. It was not a pretty sight.

This is not to condemn the celebration. What happened during the past few days will certainly go down as one of the greatest moments, if not the greatest moment, in State history. The event deserves a celebration of the highest magnitude but not a mob scene that endangers lives and property.

For those of us who were fortunate enough to attend this institution at the time the Wolfpack won its first national championship, we can be proud of that fact, and it is something we can remember and cherish for years to come. For those who suffered personal injury or property damage, the moment is somewhat tainted. Think back to what you did during the celebration, and ask yourself if you were considerate to others while celebrating the victory. Enjoying oneself and showing consideration for others can be accomplished at the same time.

Chapter 91

Others can share in State's success

Editorial reprinted from the Technician, March 27, 1974

So... it's all in the family. As Saturday's NCAA semi-final game progressed, it wasn't just those uncouth red-sneakered students from State who were on the edges of their seats. There were a lot of blue-sneakered folks going wild too. And when it was all over, it wasn't "State won." It was "We won."

That's about how it was all through the game in TV rooms across the campus: "How We doing? Do you think We can catch up? We've scored three straight now."

There was no doubt that Carolina fans, and who knows how many others across the state, had temporarily adopted the NC State team as their very own. It was UCLA versus Us.

And We finally won. Maybe it didn't mean as much as the Tar Heels beating UCLA, but at least UCLA was beaten by the only team consistently better than the Tar Heels this season.

The victory was a victory for Us for a number of reasons. It was a victory for Eastern teams, bringing the title away from Los Angeles for the first time in eight years. It was a victory for the ACC and certainly one for the State of North Carolina.

Our commendations to State, and, at the risk of sounding presumptuous, We are going to win again tonight.

*   *   *   *   *

The preceding editorial was published in Monday's *Daily Tar Heel,* and we would like to add, yes, We did win Monday night. Against UCLA and then against Marquette, the Wolfpack took on the task of representing the entire state and more. Not since Carolina took the national crown in 1957 has an Atlantic Coast Conference representative captured the NCAA championship.

Since UCLA won their first in an almost continuous string of championships back in 1964, many challengers have confronted the Bruins, and many challengers have remained just that—challengers. In the past 10 years, only the University of Texas at El Paso has managed to grab the spotlight from UCLA. After coach John Wooden began adding championship after championship to his name, many observers began to refer to the NCAA tournament as the UCLA Invitational. It took a determined effort by the Wolfpack plus a lot of faith from thousands of fans to bring the trophy back to North Carolina.

Although everybody on campus, and across the state for that matter, is currently in a period of euphoria over winning the national championship, the biggest challenge ahead of us now is to retain our humility. The university has gained a great deal of respect now. Instead of being referred to as "Cow College," State is now the NCAA national champion. To keep that respect, representatives of the university, which means you, must not become cocky and impudent. It was only a few years ago that the team was struggling to break even during the season. Even though they highlighted the campaign with a home victory over Carolina, they were eliminated in the first round of the ACC tournament. Yes, only a few seasons ago, the team epitomized the rural label accorded it.

We can bask in the limelight now, but let's not hog it (no pun intended) all to ourselves. Let's share it with others. Even though we will face each other on opposite sides of the court again next winter, we can enjoy the camaraderie of the moment now. We're number one. We're all number one.

SECTION 3

Post Championship Season

Chapter 92

In a flash, it was over

Basketball season seemed to come to an abrupt end after the Marquette game. Maybe it was because the UCLA game had so much build up and the finals were more pedestrian, but coverage of the basketball team and its accomplishments died down quickly for the *Technician* staff. There was just a month left on the academic calendar, and there were other sports to cover.

Looking back, the accomplishments of the Wolfpack over a two-year period, 1972–73 and 1973–74, were simply amazing: 57–1 overall and 24–0 in regular season conference games. Plus, State won eight other games against conference teams those two years, four in the Big Four tournament and four in the ACC tournament. State also had back-to-back years of leading the conference regular season, back-to-back ACC titles earned by winning the league tournament, and one NCAA National Championship.

We will never know if it could have been two national titles because of the probation in 1972–73 that kept the Wolfpack out of the NCAA tournament. Based on the second half performance against UCLA in December 1973, there are doubts in many minds that State could have won the title the year before. And, there are those who are confident the 1972–73 Wolfpack could have won the title. We'll never know either way.

When you see the names of the UCLA players—Bill Walton, Dave Meyers, Keith Wilkes, Tommy Curtis, Greg Lee, Marques Johnson, and Andre McCarter—who played against State in the NCAA semifinals, it makes you think at least twice about the Wolfpack's victory in the NCAA semifinals.

The same may be true about the Marquette players in the finals: Maurice Ellis, Earl Tatum, Maurice Lucas, Lloyd Walton, and Marcus Washington.

But State had players just as good or obviously better those nights:

David Thompson: 28 points and 10 rebounds against UCLA; 21 points, 7 rebounds versus Marquette.

Tommy Burleson: 20 points and 14 rebounds against UCLA; 14 points, 11 rebounds against Marquette.

Monte Towe: 12 points against UCLA and 16 against Marquette.

Tim Stoddard: 9 points, 9 rebounds, 5 assists, and 3 steals against UCLA; 8 points, 7 rebounds, and 3 steals against Marquette.

Morris Rivers: 7 points and 4 assists against UCLA; 14 points and 5 assists versus Marquette.

Those five—with steady off-the-bench defense for about 18 minutes each of those games by Phil Spence—in those two games, the hard work and fun the team had throughout the year, the adversity of the Thompson fall during the Pitt game, and the determination and fiery spirit of coach Norm Sloan pushed State to the title.

Along the way, three times State defeated both Maryland and North Carolina, two top five teams that year.

It was truly a fantastic season for Wolfpack basketball. It was a season that lingers to this day. It was, without a doubt, the best Wolfpack basketball team ever.

But, in a flash, the season was over.

Except for a couple of stories, the basketball team's accomplishments and all its glory were over and done in the *Technician*. There was no follow-up, no reliving of the title run.

But, two stories did follow shortly thereafter:

Was Monte Towe leaving State for a professional career with the Harlem Globetrotters?

Was David Thompson leaving the Wolfpack for a professional career with the NBA or ABA?

One of those stories was purposely one to fool and the other had State fans wishing and hoping it was made up.

Chapter 93

Towe inks pro contract

Reprinted from the Technician, April 1, 1974 (April Fools!)

By Steve Wheeler

Staff Writer

One of State's great basketball players will not be returning to the lineup next year. However, that player is not David Thompson, the player that many people thought would sign a pro contract after the present season was completed.

The Harlem Globetrotters yesterday announced the signing of their first white basketball player in the team's history when they signed Monte Towe off the 1974 NCAA basketball champion State Wolfpack.

The diminutive Towe, a thorn in the side of many guards in collegiate ball, has shocked the Wolfpack far and wide by inking the multi-year contract with the clowns of professional basketball. The amount of the contract was not announced but it is believed to be in the six figure range.

Some people believe that the 5'7" Converse, Indiana, native hot dogs it a bit too much on the cage court, but he would be a perfect fit with the Trotters.

Towe showed the basketball world that he could play roundball with anyone in the collegiate circuit. The scrappy guard proved his worth several times in the last two seasons, but he was never better than against UCLA. In the first game between the "kings of college basketball," Towe led the Wolfpack with 19 points, mostly on 25-foot "three pointers," and generally played his great floor game.

In the NCAA semi-finals, Towe drove the lane several times and put the ball over the outstretched arms of the best-disputed defensive player in college basketball, Bill Walton. Towe also finished this game with 19 points and caused many turnovers in the second overtime in which the Wolfpack came from 7 down in the last 3:27 of the second overtime to defeat the Bruins.

Robert Hoffman, manager of the Globetrotters, had nothing but high praise for his first white signee.

"I was afraid Towe would not sign because of the love between the members of the Wolfpack," he stated. "They really love each other. When I saw Thompson's fall in the Pittsburgh game on TV, his teammates were stunned and in tears. When he returned to the court, the players were in tears of joy. That is love.

"Towe has such a tremendous future with us," the Trotters manager said. "But the only problem is we'll have to drop 'Harlem'."

When reached for comment, Towe commented that "I hate to leave this place. I love these guys and they have given me a great three years.

"But I think my future is with the Trotters because I'm afraid the pros will overlook me because of my size. Hell, they think I am lying when I say I'm 5'7"," he said.

One of Towe's best friends ever, David Thompson said, "Monte's leaving is a tremendous loss to the team as a friend and a player."

Greg Hawkins, Towe's idol, commented, "I wish him the best of luck. Maybe he could get me a job with the Globetrotters performing at halftime standing on my hands."

Towe's leaving will be a big loss for the Pack but an asset to the Globetrotters. His leaving will also make many opposing teams happy because he will not be around gnatting their guards.

Chapter 94

Our No. 1 hope

Editorial reprinted from the Technician, April 22, 1974

An article appearing in *The Charlotte Observer* last week speculated as to whether returning to State for his senior year might cause David Thompson to miss out on signing a multi-million dollar contract to play professional basketball. It is an interesting point.

The article explained that negotiations are presently in progress that may lead to a merger between the National Basketball Association and the American Basketball Association, the two competing professional basketball leagues. If that were to happen, the bidding war to sign the top collegiate prospects that the two leagues currently engage in would be ended, and with it would go the multi-million dollar contracts that players like Thompson and Bill Walton are now being offered.

So what will David do? Well, to say the least, the student body, the faculty, the alumni, and the Pack Backers everywhere hope he will return to State for his senior year.

But the offer is no doubt a temptation to David, as it would be to anyone. If he were to sign, financial security for him and his family would be assured virtually forever. And as the eleventh of eleven children, David is well aware of the difficulty his parents have had to make ends meet over the years, and he would no doubt like to retire them to a life of comfort. David has also been forced to consider the possibility that if he were to sustain an injury next season—a distinct possibility when you play the game like he does—the big money pro contract might not be forthcoming.

Therefore, if David does sign, anyone who would criticize him for doing so would be guilty of extreme selfishness and immaturity.

But when making his decision, there is another side of the story that David should, and being the type of person he is undoubtedly will, consider. This side of the story is one of human emotion, not money.

People genuinely love and respect David Thompson, not only for his ability on a basketball court but also for being the unselfish, friendly and giving man that he has demonstrated himself to be. The outpouring of concern and prayers for David following his stunning fall in the Eastern Regionals was overwhelming. And the concern and prayers were not just for David Thompson the basketball player, they were also for David Thompson the individual.

In addition to these things, it should also be noted that the odds are probably against both an ABA-NBA merger and a Thompson injury. In fact, if David does play another year at State, he could well end up with bigger contract offers than he is receiving now.

The NBA draft will be held soon and with it will come added pressure on David to sign a pro contract. But as everyone knows, he has already voiced his intention to return to school next year.

Let's hope so.

Afterword

Well, neither Monte Towe, the subject of the well-conceived April Fool's Day edition of the *Technician,* nor David Thompson, who was rumored to be turning pro after his junior season, left State at the end of the year. Both stayed at State for a good but not championship caliber senior 1974-75 campaign in which the Wolfpack did not make the NCAA playoff field. While Towe's departure would not have happened, Thompson's could have and his staying said a lot about his desire to complete the full college basketball experience. After such a wonderful run to the NCAA title, no one could imagine Towe or Thompson passing up one more year with the Wolfpack.

When I started to write or, some may say, compile, this book, it was only about the men's basketball team for the year 1973–74. As I read and re-read the pages of the *Technician* from throughout the year, I expanded the book to include the football team and a conference championship for the Wolfpack. And, then the effort was expanded to include lots more such as student government, life outside campus, integration, Watergate, and more. I finished that effort with more than 130,000 words, and that didn't include everything at NC State that academic year.

It was fun to compile that first attempt at this book. Combining some original writing with lots of article reprints and mixing the two was somewhat creative and included, at times, some unusual and rambling writing. For instance, there was this sentence in which I summarized a stretch of baseball games that spring:

State's baseball team, coached by Sam Esposito, also an assistant basketball coach, was having its ups and downs, losing to Carolina, 8–6, at home ("We made too many errors," said Esposito after the game), then losing to Clemson, 2–1, at home after pitcher Tom Hayes allowed just two runs on eight hits ("We're very disappointed," said Esposito. "We got a great game from Tom Hayes, but they had a better pitched game"), splitting a doubleheader at Duke (pitcher Tim Stoddard walked seven and recorded six strikeouts in a 4–2 win), defeating Virginia, 8–3 (Stoddard, as the designated hitter, slammed a home run and a double, driving in two runs and scoring three times himself), picking up two wins against Wake Forest (Stoddard threw a two-hitter in the first of two, both with 3–2 final scores), then defeating Carolina, 6–2 in Chapel Hill (third baseman Ron Evans hit a three-run homer in the top of the 10th inning, upstaging two streakers wearing only Carolina caps who raced across the field during the seventh inning stretch), and losing 5–0 at Clemson. In the Clemson game, State turned a triple play as explained in the *Technician* game story: "With Clemson men taking big leads at first and second with no outs, a line drive was hit to third baseman Ron Evans and the runners started to advance. Evans caught the ball in the air and flipped it to second baseman Monte Towe for the second out. Towe then tossed it to first base where Don Zagorski tagged the bag for the third out."

Bruce Winkworth, a longtime follower of State and an excellent writer, agreed to read, critique and try to correct mistakes and actually liked the baseball sentence but suggested it be cut into pieces or not used at all: "This is essentially one sentence. Dare I suggest that it's too long by a factor of about 10?" He also said he had a hard time grasping the point of or common thread to the 130,000 word book, which was originally titled *1973–73: A life in the year at NC State University*. I had tried to make the basketball team the common thread but that just didn't work. So, the idea of condensing the words to cover just the basketball team came back to life. "But maybe that is the common thread," Bruce said, "that there is no common thread except that it's about State in the academic year 1973–74." I'm glad he picked up on that but my mind was made up to write about the real common thread.

Even after returning to the original idea of writing a book chronicling the 1973–74 basketball season as it happened through the writings in the *Technician,* I was determined to use that baseball passage, my favorite of the first complete effort. Mission accomplished.

* * * *

In researching this book—reading and re-reading the pages of the *Technician* and seeking information through various sources such as the NCAA archives, various internet searches, and State athletics publications—I came across some very interesting passages, stories and quotes that taken in context then didn't mean much more than what was on the surface, but when read today, make you pause for more consideration.

For example, Bob James was the commissioner of the ACC for 16 years, starting in the spring of 1971. He was interviewed for a story in *Touché,* the *Technician* supplement, in early September 1973, offering insights on conference formation, governance, and his opinion of the success of football and basketball in the ACC.

"At one time, the Atlantic Coast Conference was known far, far greater for its football than for its basketball," James said. "Then basketball came along, and I don't believe the opportunity of the time would ever come when our basketball would be reduced in scope. I think there is very clear evidence that our football program is coming back. It's just a matter of time."

James also looked a little into the future of the ACC. He said, "I believe there is satisfaction with the present alignment of the seven schools in the program and the type of competition we are conducting. I'm not saying there will not ever be expansion, but certainly there is none under consideration at this time."

James died in 1987. I wonder what his thoughts on the same subject would be in the year 2015.

*   *   *   *

The State basketball season—covering and writing about a championship team as a student—was a once in a lifetime treat. Helping the *Technician* staff compile the newspaper for publication three times a week was a labor of love for me and others who "worked" there. Editors, writers, typesetters, copyreaders, paste-up people, advertising sales people, and others were involved on a daily basis. Some used the work as a small but satisfying source of income. Others participated because they had a yearning for the newspaper business and this was an academic experience. If you contact anyone who worked at the *Technician* in the academic year 1973–74, to a person, they would reflect on a unique and satisfying experience, learning a trade that was not taught at State. There was no journalism school, yet the staff turned out an award-winning product. Much of our satisfaction came from the enjoyment of fellow students retrieving the newspaper Monday, Wednesday, and Friday, watching as the layouts were studied and the stories were read. The student body's reaction to our effort was as important—probably more so—than the accolades received from the professionals.

It was a fun time to be at State considering that 1973–74 was a unique year at the campus with the important role played by the basketball team as a rallying point while trouble brewed across the nation with President Richard Nixon and his growing Watergate scandal, the continuing war in Vietnam, and the burdensome oil and gas crisis gripping the country. Campus issues were just as important and consumed student interest but not as much as the basketball team did.

I had fun as a student but more so as a writer for the *Technician*.

I enjoyed looking back to compile this book. I took the initiative to glance at our life then, to chronicle some of the important things that happened at State, and then to condense the entire year into a book about one team.

It's a celebration of my youth that I give you in this volume, and I offer huge credit to the many fellow students who took time away from their academic pursuits to help me with it, not today or over the last few years but when they were students at State with me.

It was not just the basketball team that won the national championship. It was all of us there living it. With this book, we can relive 1973-74, the NC State Wolfpack's title run as it happened.

— Jim Pomeranz
NC State University '77
Sports Editor, the *Technician*,
Spring Semester 1974–Spring Semester 1975

PS—It's not over. Read the interview I conducted with David Thompson shortly after the Wolfpack's 1973–74 National Championship season.

Postscript

Interview with David Thompson

"I can be an adequate forward, maybe even a good one."

Reprinted with permission from the 1974–75 ACC Handbook

A national audience was watching. North Carolina State was hosting Maryland. And, it was Super Sunday. Although the game was tight the whole way, the Wolfpack came out on top, 80–74. Over half the points for State (41) were scored by a junior forward named David Thompson. He was super on Sunday.

There were less than seven minutes remaining on the clock, and North Carolina State's basketball team was trailing the Purdue Boilermakers by 15 points. The Wolfpack called time and a conference was held around State's bench. The Pack just couldn't lose this game. The strategy decided upon was— give the ball to David. The reasoning worked out, and State won, 86–81. David, who had gone scoreless in the first 16 minutes of play, sparked the win with 26 points.

"David was tremendous," raved State head coach Norm Sloan after the Wolfpack had handed Maryland its third conference loss of the season and the second by State, 86–80. Thompson tossed in 39 points in College Park, MD that night.

"David Thompson is no 'superman'" proclaimed the article. But then it backed up and said concerning leaping over tall buildings in a single bound that "with a running jump, all bets are off." He didn't try it, but he might have made it.

David Thompson, All-America for two years and the Associated Press Player of the Year in 1974, has walked, talked, eaten, and slept basketball on the North Carolina State campus for the past three years. And throughout his Wolfpack career, he has carried State to victory numerous times.

Considered by many as the greatest college basketball player ever, the 6'4" guard-forward-center all rolled into one, has dazzled basketball fans worldwide.

Not only have fans in Raleigh and throughout the ACC applauded Thompson's roundball skills but   fans in Moscow, Munich, Manila, and Tokyo as well. His talents have taken him to the court against such greats as those on the Russian National team, and he and his teammates have still come out the victors. David Thompson will probably go down in history as one of the most complete and one of the greatest basketball players ever.

The senior from Shelby, NC, has just one more year of collegiate ball to play before he takes his talents to the professional ranks.

The following interview with Thompson is by Jim Pomeranz, sports editor of the Technician, North Carolina State University's student newspaper. It delves into just a small but interesting part of Thompson's life.

JIM POMERANZ: Tell me about the first time you ever picked up a basketball.

DAVID THOMPSON: Well, the first time I remember picking up a basketball, I was about seven years old. It was in my backyard. My brother, who was seven years older and in high school at the time, built a basketball court behind the house. I was out playing with him and some of his friends.

POMERANZ: When you started playing at the age of seven did you have any thoughts of how you would be in the future?

THOMPSON: No, not at that time, but it didn't take me very long to catch on to basketball. I played just about every day, and I enjoyed it. So I felt that I could continue playing hopefully in high school at the time.

POMERANZ: When did you really start playing in some sort of organized basketball?

THOMPSON: Well, the first time that I played on an organized basketball team was when I was in the ninth grade. I played on the junior varsity that year. But then by the end of the season during the tournament time, they moved me up to the varsity team. I guess I was the star on the JV team. I was the leading scorer, and rebounder, and assist man.

POMERANZ: When you moved up to the varsity, what was your reaction?

THOMPSON: Well, it made me feel pretty good. It gave me a feeling of accomplishment, you know. And it gave me something to shoot for next year, my sophomore year, as for gaining a starting position on the varsity.

POMERANZ: Did you gain that starting position the next year on the varsity?

THOMPSON: Yes, I did. I started on the varsity every game, and I was the leading scorer on the team and the third leading scorer in the conference. I think I averaged around 20 points per game that year.

POMERANZ: What about your rebounding, and what position did you play?

THOMPSON: I played guard and forward. I was the leading rebounder on the team too.

POMERANZ: Who was the tallest man on the team, and how tall was he?

THOMPSON: We had a 6'7" guy by the name of Barry Ledbetter who went on to play at Western Carolina.

POMERANZ: Who could jump higher, you or him?

THOMPSON: At the time, it was about even. He could jump pretty good.

POMERANZ: Could you pinpoint a few reasons why you decided to come to North Carolina State?

THOMPSON: One reason was that the year before they had signed Tom Burleson, who is 7'4" and a nucleus for any team. And since winning was my main goal, I felt that playing with a guy that big along with the other freshmen they signed that year and the older players, eventually NC State would have the chance to win the national championship. And also, I enjoy how the players communicated with the coaches and the relationship they had with one another. Those were the basic things that led me to sign with State.

POMERANZ: In your freshman year, you lost one game; that was to North Carolina.

THOMPSON: Ha-ha-ha!

POMERANZ: And in your sophomore year, your first year on the Wolfpack varsity, you made All-American.

THOMPSON: That's right!

POMERANZ: Do you think you deserved that honor?

THOMPSON: Yeah, I thought I deserved it, you know. I put in a lot of hard work, but I really felt that I wasn't that much better than any of the other players. It was just the situation that made me stand out. I had a lot of teammates that got me the ball: Monte Towe, Joe Cafferky, Tim Stoddard, and the other guys. That helped out a lot. That made it that much easier for me. I think that any time you play on a team that goes undefeated, a few of the players are going to get national recognition, and I happened to be one of the players.

POMERANZ: At the end of that year with the team's record 27–0 and State unable to go to any postseason tournaments, how did you feel?

THOMPSON: I felt that we got a raw deal. The reasons that we got put on probation were not really adequate enough, as far as I was concerned, to place any team on probation. At the end of the season, I felt empty. I guess they gave us an incentive to play that much harder next year and to prove to everybody that going 27–0, we had the capabilities of winning the national championship the year before.

POMERANZ: During your junior year, State won the national championship, and you were once again All-America and named the Associated Press Player of the Year. Could you give a brief overview of the season on your play as well as the whole team's play?

THOMPSON: I thought the team started out a little slower than it should, and I thought I started out a little slower than I should have too. But we had new players that played a big role in our winning, and it took us time to adjust to each other. Morris Rivers and Phil Spence played an important role in our winning the national championship. It took time for them to blend in their talents with the talents we already had and vice versa.

POMERANZ: During the Eastern Regionals, you took a bad fall in Reynolds Coliseum and hurt yourself. Can you remember anything about the leap before the fall?

THOMPSON: No, I can't. I can only remember the play before that, but after that, it was total darkness for a while. The next thing I can remember is waking up in the ambulance with my mother beside me.

POMERANZ: When you returned to the Coliseum later and the game was still going on, you received a tremendous response from the crowd. What was your reaction to this?

THOMPSON: It was really touching. It was probably the greatest feeling I've ever felt. I can't really describe it. It really showed love by the people. It really made it all worthwhile, you know. It was fantastic. That will probably be one of the things I remember the most about my college career, about the way the people reacted to me being injured. They were really concerned about me as a person and not only as a ball player.

POMERANZ: Do you ever worry about getting hurt while playing basketball?

THOMPSON: No, I don't worry about getting hurt. I just go out and play my regular game. That just happened that one time. You always take a chance when you play. I think if I were to be afraid of getting hurt, it would hurt my game.

POMERANZ: How much time in the off-season would you normally spend playing basketball?

THOMPSON: We play just about every day except on Sundays. We play about an hour and a half to two hours a day.

POMERANZ: Do you ever get bored with basketball?

THOMPSON: Sometimes you get a little tired, but you never get bored with it because it is a game that you love, a game that you enjoy playing. It's a lot of fun playing basketball if you really get into it.

POMERANZ: Do you ever get tired of talking basketball?

THOMPSON: Well, no. Basketball is a part of me, and by it being a part of me, I don't mind talking about basketball. Sometimes, it goes to an extreme for some people. Generally, I enjoy talking about it.

POMERANZ: What was the toughest game you have ever played in your life?

THOMPSON: Probably the most demanding game I played in was against Maryland in the ACC tournament. It was really draining. It drained me mentally and physically. It was a tight, suspenseful game the whole way through. At the end of the game, I felt I had played eight games that one night. It was really tiring.

POMERANZ: What player has defended you the best, and what player has given you the most trouble when you were on defense?

THOMPSON: Bobby Jones (of Carolina) defended me as well as anyone, probably he and Keith Wilkes (of UCLA) did the best job on me. And probably the toughest guy for me to defend was Keith Wilkes.

POMERANZ: Other than the incident that was so publicized about you signing a professional contract with the NBA Philadelphia 76ers, have there been any more pressures from pro teams for you to sign?

THOMPSON: No, not really. That was the only time that has happened.

POMERANZ: There have been no pressures from individuals about signing pro contracts?

THOMPSON: No. You get agents that come in and talk to you pretty much. I had an incident where the same guy kept pestering me. Even though I would tell him that I wasn't interested, he would keep coming back. That's about the only thing like that that has happened.

POMERANZ: What are your thoughts about losing that game to North Carolina during your freshman year?

THOMPSON: Probably the main reason we lost that game was because a lot of our big men got into foul trouble in the second half and fouled out with a lot of time left. In that particular game, we were leading by 15 points at the half. Carolina had a big front line: Donald Washington, Ed Stahl, Mickey Bell, and some other players. They just out-boarded us after Tim Stoddard fouled out. I was about the tallest guy in the game at the end for State.

POMERANZ: With your great leaping ability, have you had to play the center position or jump center other than in the USA-USSR series?

THOMPSON: I played a little center my junior year in high school, but I've never really had to play center. That's not the position to utilize my best talents.

POMERANZ: What about the loss to UCLA?

THOMPSON: Well, I think we got tired a little bit, and when we got behind, we didn't have too much organization. We just fell apart really.

POMERANZ: Did you have any plans made for the terrific amount of money you will get for signing a pro contract when you do sign?

THOMPSON: First of all, I would like to help my parents and my relatives, and after that, I really don't have any outlandish plans. I don't want to build a million-dollar house like Wilt Chamberlain or anything like that.

POMERANZ: In the past, you have mentioned something about wanting to open sports camps. Could you elaborate a little?

THOMPSON: When I was growing up, around my area there weren't enough facilities to play in. I would look for some place to play, and I couldn't find a place to play in the whole town. I think there is a need for more in every area for anybody. We played at a high school gym, and it wasn't open on the weekends or anything like that. The only time it was open was when Coach Peeler came and opened the gym. In order to be a good athlete, you have got to play every day, especially when you're little. You have to come out and work your ass off. I think a lot of kids would benefit by that.

POMERANZ: Speaking of your family, you are the ninth child in your family, aren't you?

THOMPSON: No, I'm the eleventh.

POMERANZ: How many brothers do you have?

THOMPSON: Three.

POMERANZ: And you have seven sisters?

THOMPSON: Right.

POMERANZ: How can you live with all those girls?

THOMPSON: They took care of me. I didn't have to do any chores.

POMERANZ: What are your brothers and sisters doing now?

THOMPSON: Most of them are married and working. Most of them moved up north. Most of my relatives live around the Washington, DC, area.

POMERANZ: Do you ever get to visit them, or do they ever get to come down to Raleigh to see any games?

THOMPSON: Yes, they come down to see some games, and they catch all the Maryland games. We just had a family reunion recently. We had everybody together.

POMERANZ: Speaking of Maryland, what is your opinion surrounding Moses Malone, his commitment to Maryland, and then his switch to pro ball? Was this a wise decision?

THOMPSON: I don't really have any say so on that because either way, he would be making pretty nice. He signed a nice contract. But then again, I thought that one or two years of college experience would help him a lot more.

POMERANZ: Do you think there are recruiting rules that need to be changed?

THOMPSON: Well, I only have one. I think the number of visits that a coach can visit a prospect should be limited. It would help out as far as some of the confusion surrounding recruiting is concerned.

POMERANZ: Is one visit adequate enough?

THOMPSON: No, I think maybe five by the school, not by one coach but by the school.

POMERANZ: What about visits to the school?

THOMPSON: Well, I think it is pretty good now.

POMERANZ: What kind of approach would you take when recruiting a David Thompson?

THOMPSON: First, I would see what type of academic field he wanted to get into. Then I would introduce him to the players and let him mingle with the players and see if he could relate to the type of atmosphere and the types of attitudes the players have. I think that's real important, the attitudes. I think one player with a bad attitude could destroy a whole team.

POMERANZ: What kind of relationship do you have with the other members of State's team?

THOMPSON: Everybody is real close. We do a lot of things together, and by everybody being close like that, it helps us on the court because we are friends. And that way, you don't have two guys working with themselves and three other guys working together. Everybody is working for that one cause, which is winning.

POMERANZ: What about your relationship with coach Norm Sloan and his staff?

THOMPSON: We've got a real good relationship. We talk like men. We bring our problems to focus and discuss a lot of different things. We all consider ourselves persons so we relate on that level.

POMERANZ: When you are at practice, is coach Sloan able to help you with your game? Does he see a flaw in your movement and help you change it?

THOMPSON: Coaches are real important. Their main goal is to get the team organized and keep them under a certain framework. But then if a coach knows a certain flaw, he will pick it up pretty quickly and tell you about it so you can work on it. Since I've been here, he has seen a lot of flaws in the way I play, and I think by him coaching me, he's told me the right things to do and helped me out and made me a lot better ball player.

POMERANZ: What do you do to get away from the activity that surrounds you at State?

THOMPSON: Nothing special, really. I just come back to my room and listen to music and do some studying.

POMERANZ: What kind of music do you like?

THOMPSON: Different types, it all depends on the mood I'm in.

POMERANZ: What other interests do you have? Do you play any other sports?

THOMPSON: I like to play other sports but don't really have the time. I'm basically a spectator. I enjoy football and enjoy going to all the football games. And I enjoy baseball.

POMERANZ: Do you like to go to movies?

THOMPSON: Yeah, pretty much.

POMERANZ: What about reading books?

THOMPSON: I enjoy books, but I really don't have much time except for the basic academic books. I like to shoot pool.

POMERANZ: What kind of pool shooter are you? Are you pretty good?

THOMPSON: I'm all right.

POMERANZ: Can you whip all the other members of the basketball team?

THOMPSON: Most of them, except Stoddard. He's pretty tough.

POMERANZ: Have you been shooting pool for a long time?

290

THOMPSON: Well, yeah, I've been shooting pretty long. I didn't really start shooting seriously until I was 15 or 16.

POMERANZ: About this year's (1974–75) team, will Phil Spence be playing center for State?

THOMPSON: Probably, Spence and Stoddard will be rotating at center. When one is playing center, the other will be playing forward. Sure, there is a problem there (with the height difference from Burleson to Spence), but the way we have to alter our game is to use more quickness and a lot more pressure defense.

POMERANZ: What type of offense will State throw at opponents this year?

THOMPSON: We'll have a freelance offense, which will be a lot of movement—passing and cutting—basically the same offense we had last year with the exception that this year, we are going to add more screening away from the ball. It's just gonna be more movement where we're gonna move the ball around real fast and everybody is moving to the open spot. Whoever is open gets the shot. It won't be an offense where we come down and play one-on-one, like that. Since we don't have a set offense, everybody thinks we just have five individual one-on-one players, but it's not like that. It's a team oriented offense. But from it comes a lot of one-on-one play. Under certain circumstances you isolate players—say myself, Monte Towe could go one-on-one, and Moe Rivers. We have the type of players that can do that. But basically, we will be running an offense similar to the Boston Celtics with a lot of movement and a lot of picking away from the ball.

POMERANZ: Do you prefer a man-to-man defense or a zone defense?

THOMPSON: I prefer a man-to-man defense because you can do a lot of different things against a man-to-man, and it's not as congested in the middle. Personally, a lot of my game is driving to the basket and an inside game, but when you play against a zone, that clogs it up. You have three or four guys right in there in the middle plus you have your own teammates in there, and you really don't have that much working room. Mostly your game will be an outside game. The best way to offense against a zone defense is to overload one side and swing the ball quickly to the other side for that short jumper.

POMERANZ: There were times during last season that the offense seemed to be "give the ball to David" and let him score. Have there been times that you have had to carry the team, and do you feel any added pressures at those tunes?

THOMPSON: Well, I don't really feel like I have to carry the team. And I don't feel any added pressure either. But under certain circumstances—and I think all players have a lot of confidence in themselves—and in a clutch situation, I like to be the one with the ball. I think Monte Towe and other guys are the same way too. It all depends on who has the hot hand. If you have the hot hand, then quite naturally, they are going to go to you. A lot of times you initiate the action because everybody gets the ball, and they feel that you have the shot because you go ahead and cause some type of action to either get a shot or pass off for two points.

POMERANZ: Would you like to see the dunk come back into collegiate basketball?

THOMPSON: Yeah, I would. It's a spectacular play. The fans really like it. I really enjoyed playing against the Russians and during the Oriental tour because we could dunk. It made you play that much harder and work that much harder to get inside and get open, and everybody is running to the boards for tip-ins and stuff like that. It's

292

an exciting play. I think everybody would want the dunk back in college basketball.

POMERANZ: During last year when the "alley-oop" play came about, were there times when you were above the basket that you just wanted to flip it down into the basket at a harder rate than just dropping it in the basket?

THOMPSON: Yeah, well at times under certain circumstances, it's best to dunk, but then it's illegal. A couple of times last year, I got called for offensive goal tending. One particular time against North Carolina, I had the lob pass, and Bobby Jones swung at the ball, and I threw it down a little too hard. If you were able to dunk, that would be two points there. I think that if the dunk rule was in basketball, it would have helped Tom Burleson out a lot because he missed a lot of little easy two foot shots, whereas he could have otherwise dunked them in. He missed them because he didn't want to put his hands in the perimeter and be called for offensive goal tending.

POMERANZ: Where would you like to play in pro ball, guard or forward? Where are you better?

THOMPSON: I don't really know. I've never played guard that much. And I don't know how I'll do in pro ball. But I feel that I could play forward. I could be an adequate forward, maybe even a good one. And I feel that I would be the type of ball player similar to John Havlicek, the type that could play guard or forward. That would be beneficial in certain different circumstances. Say you play a team that has two big guards, and they are killing a short guard. Then they could use me at guard. Say we play a team with some small quick forwards. Then I would be of value at forward. But I think my best position is forward. I'm a natural at forward; I've played it almost all my life. People compare me with Charlie Scott, but there's quite a big difference there. Charlie Scott is a guard who can play forward. I'm a forward who can play guard.

POMERANZ: Do you have an idol in sports?

THOMPSON: Well, I really like Dr. Julius Erving. I think he's got a good image for young kids. He's really a nice guy, a down to earth fellow, and he's a great ball player. I think he's had a great influence on kids, young kids, as far as being basketball players are concerned. He's a great guy. He does a lot of little things like taking time to sign autographs and stuff like that that really mean a lot to an eight- or nine-year-old kid.

POMERANZ: Do you think State can win the national championship again this year?

THOMPSON: Yeah, I think we can. I think our chances are as good as anybody else's.

POMERANZ: Who else do you consider as a contender? A lot of people consider other schools in the ACC.

THOMPSON: Maryland is a contender, and Carolina could possibly be, I think. UCLA will be strong as will Indiana and probably Purdue.

POMERANZ: Do you think State will finish first in the ACC?

THOMPSON: I hope so. It's hard to say this early. It all depends on how the games go at the beginning of the season. But our main goal is winning the ACC tournament.

POMERANZ: Who do you think will be the first to defeat State this year?

THOMPSON: I don't think any team will whip us. That's hard to answer because we could possibly go undefeated again. But probably Maryland will have the best chance to beat us.

POMERANZ: Basketball aside, what are your feelings about black and white relationships today?

THOMPSON: I think the situation is getting better, but we still have a long way to go because there are a lot of narrow-minded people. People get more open. I think by whites and blacks being around each other more, that's helped the problem because they found out, "Wow, he's a person just like I am," and "he has feelings the same as I do." The only difference between you and me is probably physical differences.

Overtime

The Stuff of Memories

Sometime in the mid-1990s, and I'm not sure where it was other than in Cary NC, a gentleman about my age approached me with a huge grin on his face. He extended his right hand and offered a shake. "Do you remember me?" he asked.

I hesitated for what seemed like an eternity though it was only seconds. "Not really," I answered. I could not place him at all. But he was greeting me as he would a long-lost friend. He was excited to see me, but I couldn't figure out why. "Who are you?" I asked.

"I'm the guy you picked up on the highway in Greensboro after the 1974 game against Marquette," he said. "You picked me up. I was hitch-hiking. My ride had left me, and I was trying to get back to campus."

Then, at that moment, it all came back to me. I vividly remembered the night, that ride home, and his thanking me profusely as he exited the car. "How'd you do on the test that day?" I asked, chuckling a little.

"I failed the heck out of it," he said. "Made a 50 or something like that."

"But that didn't stop you," I said, recognizing his name associated with a local, successful engineering firm.

"No, but it's sort of funny what happened a few years later," he said. "The professor, a transportation professor, gave me no slack. I told him I was going to the game and asked if I could take the test some other time. He wouldn't allow it. But, then, after I started this engineering firm, we hired that professor to do a traffic study. He agreed for a $5,000 fee. After the study was completed, he came to our office to pick up his check. I took him into the conference room and told him what he had done to me when I was a student. He said he didn't remember and that he would have never done that. But I remembered and produced the actual test, dated and graded. I told him pay back was tough, then pulled out a $5,000 check and tore it up in front of him. He was shocked. Then I pulled out the real check and gave it to him."

My friend and I laughed at his story; then we relived that night (or early morning) in 1974. His was a story he had told and retold many times to others since it had happened. It was and is all woven into the fabric of that special time—winning the national championship, the chance of picking him up for a ride back to Raleigh, the failed test, the shock on his professor's face when he tore up the check. He's told it more since our chance meeting about 20 years after the fact. Every time he sees me, he approaches and relates the story to anyone who will listen. We laugh and joke about it. It's stuff you just can't make up. It's now more than a memory; for me, it is part of the overall story.

The 1973–74 NC State basketball season provided me great memories of the games and behind-the-scene stories of the players and coaches—some that went untold, at least in the *Technician*. For instance, there was the time coach Norm Sloan tried to toss me from the charter flight to Purdue, and then, after arriving, tried to leave me at the airport instead of welcoming me on the team bus to the hotel, all in the wake of the Morris Rivers aspirin incident and reporting thereof in the *Technician.* Thanks to then associate athletics director Frank Weedon for subduing Coach Sloan.

There were the parties around campus frequented by the players, late night high-jinx and other "fun" times. The stories told and retold today by the members of the 1973–74 State team will live as long as they do. Those conversations would make for very interesting and entertaining reading, but that's not what this book is about.

This book is about a great year in college basketball by the NC State men's basketball team. In my humble opinion, it was the greatest season ever for the Wolfpack, surpassing all that came before and every season and team that came and will come after. To me, it's about the memories; the story about stopping to pick up a stranger was just one of them. Every time I see my friend Tony Withers, we relive that night and the early morning and the special year we both enjoyed at NC State. It was indeed an extraordinary championship season, one to be remembered and relived forever. Go Pack!

—Jim Pomeranz

Acknowledgments

Thanks go out to many people but only a few can be named here.

To Ken Lloyd who was the sports editor who promoted me from *Technician* staff writer to assistant sports editor in the fall of 1973. And, to Beverly Privette, *Technician* editor for promoting me to sports editor in spring 1974, making this book possible.

To A.C. Snow, then associate editor of the *Raleigh Times,* who was the *Technician* advisor for his critique of my writings during my early years at NC State. He remains today a trusted grammar guru.

To Ivan Mothershead who asked me to interview David Thompson for Ivan's first *ACC Basketball Handbook* (1974-75). It may not have helped sell magazines, but it is a plus to have now.

To Eddie Biedenbach who lived the championship season as it happened and who took the time to relive it with me through conversations and his Foreword.

To Bruce Winkworth, a multi-year staff writer for the *Technician* and a Wolfpack historian who was the first content editor for this book and offered sage advice. Some was taken; some not.

Thanks to Marie Dvorak and Maggie Pagratis who helped me more than I ever expected with the editing of and the nuts and bolts of designing and publishing of my first book.

And, a special shout out to my roommates and friends at Kings Row Apartments in Raleigh, 1973-74: Jim Frisbie, Tim Leith, and Bob McSwain. It was a fun year! I hope you relive it as well.

1973-74 NC STATE PLAYER AND TEAM STATISTICS

Record: Overall, Won 30, Lost 1; ACC: 14-0

First Row: (left to right): manager Mike Sloan, Steve Smoral, Craig Kuszmaul, Mark Moeller, Monte Towe, David Thompson, Greg Hawkins, Morris Rivers, Bruce Dayhuff.
Second Row: Assistant coach Eddie Biedenbach, Assistant coach Art Musselman, Steve Nuce, Dwight Johnson, Jerry Hunt, Tim Stoddard, Steve Smith, Ken Gehring, Assistant coach Sam Esposito, Head coach Norman Sloan.
Third Row: Bill Lake, Tommy Burleson, Phil Spence, Mike Buurma. (Photo by Burnie Batchelor)

1973-74 NC STATE WOLFPACK												High
Player	G	FGM-FGA	Pct.	FTM-FTA	Pct.	Reb.	Avg.	PF	Disq.	Pts.	Avg.	Game
David Thompson	31	325-594	.547	155-208	.745	245	7.9	79	2	805	26.0	41
Tommy Burleson	31	228-442	.516	106-162	.654	377	12.2	93	2	562	18.1	38
Monte Towe	31	168-325	.517	60-74	.811	67	2.2	82	0	396	12.8	21
Morris Rivers	30	155-320	.484	53-81	.654	86	2.9	87	2	363	12.1	24
Phil Spence	30	74-149	.497	32.52	.615	188	6.3	48	1	180	6.0	14
Tim Stoddard	31	74-178	.416	23-33	.697	141	4.6	93	5	171	5.5	16
Steve Nuce	28	51-110	.464	22-28	.786	89	3.2	50	1	124	4.4	13
Mark Moeller	30	30-69	.435	21-23	.913	36	1.2	30	0	81	2.7	8
Greg Hawkins	25	23-49	.469	25-34	.735	36	1.4	27	0	71	2.8	8
Dwight Johnson	19	9-18	.500	11-18	.611	13	0.7	16	0	29	1.5	10
Bill Lake	14	6-16	.375	3-5	.600	11	0.8	5	0	15	1.1	4
Steve Smith	8	3-4	.750	1-2	.500	5	0.6	5	0	7	0.9	2
Ken Gehring	8	2-6	.333	1-2	.500	4	0.5	1	0	5	0.6	2
Mike Buurma	13	3-14	.214	1-2	.500	7	0.5	5	0	7	0.5	3
Craig Kuszmaul	18	3-8	.375	2.5	.400	6	0.3	9	0	8	0.4	4
Bruce Dayhuff	16	2.14	.143	3.4	.750	6	0.4	4	0	7	0.4	4
Jerry Hunt	5	1-3	.333	0-0	.000	1	0.2	0	0	2	0.4	2
STATE TOTALS	31	1157-2319	.499	519-733	.708	1452	46.8	634	13	2833	91.4	113
OPPONENTS	31	957-2198	.435	403-608	.663	1249	40.3	691	28	2317	74.7	100

1973-74 NC STATE GAME-BY-GAME RESULTS

Record: Overall, Won 30, Lost 1; ACC: 14-0

Date	Opponent (rank*)	Site	W/L: Score	High Scorer	High Rebounder
Dec 5	East Carolina (2, NR)	H	W: 79-47	Thompson 28	Burleson 13
Dec 7	Vermont (2, NR)	H	W: 97-42	Thompson 19	Burleson 11
Dec 15	UCLA (2,1) in St Louis	N	L: 84-66	Thompson 17	Burleson 15
Dec 18	Georgia (5, NR)	H	W: 94-60	Thompson 28	Spence 15
Sugar Bowl Tournament at New Orleans (two games)					
Dec 28	Villanova (5, NR)	N	W: 97-82	Thompson 26	Burleson 12
Dec 29	Memphis State (5, 18)	N	W: 98-83	Thompson 34	Burleson 15
Big Four Tournament at Greensboro Coliseum (two games)					
Jan 4	North Carolina (5, 4)	N	W: 78-77	Burleson 22	Burleson 14
Jan 5	Wake Forest (5, NR)	N	W: 91-73	Burleson 23	Burleson 9
Jan 12	Clemson (4, NR)	H	W: 96-68	Towe 19	Nuce 7
Jan 13	Maryland (4, 3)	H	W: 80-74	Thompson 41	Burleson 10
Jan 17	Virginia (3, NR)	A	W: 90-70	Thompson 30	Burleson 13
Jan 19	UNC-Charlotte (3, NR)	H	W: 104-72	Burleson 29	Burleson 10
Jan 22	North Carolina (3, 4)	A	W: 83-80	Thompson 26	Burleson 11
Jan 26	Purdue (3, NR)	A	W: 86-81	Thompson 26	Burleson 17
Jan 30	Maryland (2, 6)	A	W: 86-80	Thompson 39	Burleson 13
Feb 2	Virginia (2, NR)	H	W: 105-93	Thompson 23	Burleson 13
Feb 4	Duke (2, NR)	A	W: 92-78	Thompson 23	Burleson 15
North-South Doubleheader at Charlotte Coliseum (two games)					
Feb 8	Georgia Tech (2, NR)	N	W: 98-54	Towe 21	Burleson 12
Feb 9	Furman (2, NR)	N	W: 111-91	Thompson 26	Burleson 10
Feb 13	Davidson (2, NR)	H	W: 105-78	Rivers 24	Burleson, Spence 7
Feb 16	Wake Forest (2, NR)	H	W: 111-96	Thompson 31	Burleson, Thompson 12
Feb 20	Duke (1, NR)	H	W: 113-87	Thompson 40	Thompson 14
Feb 23	Clemson (1, NR)	A	W: 80-75	Thompson 35	Burleson 10
Feb 26	North Carolina (1, 4)	H	W: 83-72	Burleson 22	Burleson 11
Mar 2	Wake Forest (1, NR)	H	W: 72-63	Thompson 21	Burleson 16
ACC TOURNAMENT at Greensboro Coliseum (two games)					
Mar 8	Virginia (1, NR)	N	W: 87-66	Thompson 37	Spence 13
Mar 9	Maryland* (1, 5)	N	W: 103-100 (OT)	Burleson 38	Burleson 13
NCAA EASTERN REGIONALS at Reynolds Coliseum, Raleigh (two games)					
Mar 14	Providence (Semis) (1, 5)	H	W: 92-78	Thompson 40	Burleson 24
Mar 16	Pittsburgh (Finals) (1, 13)	H	W: 100-72	Burleson 26	Spence 14
NCAA CHAMPIONSHIP at Greensboro Coliseum (two games)					
Mar 23	UCLA** (Semis) (1, 2)	N	W: 80-77 (2OT)	Thompson 28	Burleson 14
Mar 25	Marquette (Finals) (1, 3)	N	W: 76-64	Thompson 21	Burleson 11

Rank*: NC State rank followed by opponents rank at time of game; NR (not ranked)

Site: H (home); A (at opponent); N (neutral site as noted)

About the front cover

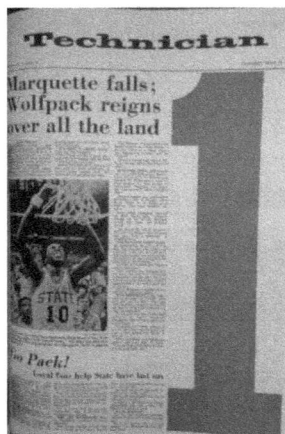

TEE-SHIRT: The background of the cover is a tee-shirt purchased by author Jim Pomeranz not long after the Wolfpack won the 1974 NCAA national title. The shirt is now in the possession of Jim's daughter, avid NC State fan. The backdrop is the wooden floor in her apartment, giving the appearance of a basketball court. An iPhone 5 was used to take the tee-shirt photo.

TECHNICIAN #1: The front page of the *Technician*, Wednesday, March 27, 1974 edition is shown on the left and right of the strip of four images. For its use, a photograph of that page was taken by author Jim Pomeranz with an iPhone 5.

DAVID THOMPSON: Both photos by Ed Caram, *Technician* staff photographer. On the left, Thompson leaps above UCLA's Bill Walton and Keith Wilkes in the NCAA semi-finals. On the right, Thompson flashes "#1" after the State defeated Marquette for the national title. Both photos were given by Caram to then sports editor Jim Pomeranz after publication in the March 25 and 27, 1974 editions of the *Technician*. Caram, who had an amazing knack for taking story-telling photos, passed away at age 66, September 1, 2013.

About the Author

Jim Pomeranz is a 1977 graduate of NC State University, a native of Sanford NC, and an avid and lifetime Wolfpack fan. He ventured into journalism early in his college career, reporting on intramural athletics for the student newspaper, *Technician,* writing his way from staff writer to assistant sports editor and to sports editor and serving in that position when the Wolfpack basketball team won the 1974 NCAA national championship. Following graduation, Pomeranz worked in the sports information department of the NCSU department of athletics and for the Wolfpack Club, 1977-87, as publications editor overseeing content and publishing of the basketball and football media guides and game programs. Along with being at courtside for the 1974 title game, Pomeranz was also at courtside when the Wolfpack won the 1983 NCAA championship. While a student, while working at State and for a few more years, he covered Atlantic Coast Conference basketball and other topics for United Press International. This book, *1973-74 Reliving the NC State Wolfpack's Title Run,* is Pomeranz's first published book. As a student writer and sports editor, Pomeranz followed in the footsteps of his father, Robert E. (Bob) Pomeranz (NCSU '43) who also wrote for the Technician and was sports editor, 1941-42.

www.ingramcontent.com/pod-product-compliance
Lightning Source LLC
Chambersburg PA
CBHW030413100426
42812CB00028B/2948/J